Published in 2016 by:
Helion & Company Limited
26 Willow Road
Solihull
West Midlands
B91 1UE
England
Tel. 0121 705 3393
Fax 0121 711 4075
email: info@helion.co.uk
website: www.helion.co.uk
Twitter: @helionbooks
Visit our blog http://blog.helion.co.uk/

Text © Aaron Morris 2016
Photographs © as individually credited
Colour profiles/artworks © Tom Cooper and
    Ugo Crisponi 2015
Maps and Unit Insignia © Helion & Company
    Limited. Drawn by George Anderson

Designed & typeset by Farr out Publications,
    Wokingham, Berkshire
Cover design by Farr out Publications,
    Wokingham, Berkshire
Printed by Henry Ling Limited, Dorchester,
    Dorset

ISBN 978-1-910294-06-2

British Library Cataloguing-in-Publication
Data
A catalogue record for this book is available
from the British Library

Cover: Force of well-armed MNLF insurgents
armed with a G–3 and M14 assault rifles, M1
Carbines and several M16A1s. In terms of
small–unit armament, insurgents are often
better armed than AFP units of comparable
size.

CONTENTS

ABBREVIATIONS

AA	anti–aircraft
AAA	Anti–Aircraft Artillery
AAM	Air–to–Air Missile
AB	Air Base
AB	Agusta–Bell (Italian manufacturer of helicopters)
ACS	Air Commando Squadron
AFP	Armed Forces of the Philippines
APC	Armoured Personnel Carrier
AS	Attack Squadron
ASG	Abu Sayyaf Group
ATGM	anti–tank guided missile
BAC	British Aircraft Corporation
BAe	British Aerospace
BAR	Browning Automatic Rifle
BCT	Battalion Combat Team
BIFF	Bangomoro Islamic Freedom Fighters (extremist Islamist insurgent movement)
Brig Gen	Brigadier General (military commissioned officer rank)
CAP	Combat Air Patrol
Capt	Captain (military commissioned officer rank)
CAS	Close Air Support
CBU	cluster bomb unit
CIA	Central Intelligence Agency (USA)
C–in–C	Chief–in–Command
c/n	construction number
CO	Commanding Officer
COIN	Counterinsurgency
Col	Colonel (military commissioned officer rank)
ECM	Electronic countermeasures
ELINT	Electronic intelligence
FAC	Forward Air Controller
Flt Lt	Flight Lieutenant (military commissioned officer rank, equal to Captain)
FMS	Foreign Military Sales
FW	Fighter Wing
FS	Fighter Squadron
GCI	ground control/ed interception
Gen	General (military commissioned officer rank)
GP	General–purpose (bomb)
HDFG(A)	Home Defence Forces Group (Airborne)
HE	high explosive
HMB	Hukbong Mapagpalaya ng Bayan (Huk Armed Forces, insurgent organization)
HQ	headquarters
HVT	High Value Target
ICRC	International Committee of the Red Cross
IFF	Identification Friend or Foe
IB	Infantry Battalion
ID	Infantry Division
IR	Infra–red, electromagnetic radiation longer than deepest red light sensed as heat
IP	Instructor Pilot
ISF	Internal Security Force
JSOTF–P	Joint Special Operations Task Force Philippines
KIA	killed in action
Km	kilometre
Lt	Lieutenant (military commissioned officer rank)

Lt Col	Lieutenant–Colonel (military commissioned officer rank)
1st Lt	First Lieutenant (military commissioned officer rank)
2nd Lt	Second Lieutenant (lowest military commissioned officer rank)
LRB	Light Reaction Battalion
LRC	Light Reaction Company
LRR	Light Reaction Regiment
Maj	Major (military commissioned officer rank)
Maj Gen	Major–General (military commissioned officer rank)
MANPADS	man–portable air defence system(s) – light surface–to–air missile system that can be carried and deployed in combat by a single soldier
MAP	Military Assistance Program ()
MBLT	Marine Battalion Landing Team
MIS	Military Intelligence Service
MHz	Megahertz, millions of cycles per second
Mi	Mil (Soviet/Russian helicopter designer and manufacturer)
MIA	missing in action
MIB	Mechanized Infantry Battalion
MILF	Moro Islamic Liberation Front (separatist extremist Islamist insurgent movement)
MNLF	Moro National Liberation Front (separatist insurgent movement)
MoD	Ministry of Defence
MRC	Marine Recon Company
MRAP	Mine resistant, ambush–protected vehicle
MSSR	Marine Scout Sniper Rifle ()
Nav/attack	Used for navigation and to aim weapons against surface target
NAMC	National Aero Manufacturing Corporation ()
NCO	Non–commissioned officer
NPA	New People's Army
OCU	Operational Conversion Unit
OEF	Operation Enduring Freedom
ORBAT	Order of Battle
PA	Philippine Army
PAAC	Philippines Army Air Corps
PC	Philippine Constabulary
PhAF	Philippine Air Force
PMC	Philippine Marine Corps
PMRF	Philippine Marine Ready Force
PN	Philippine Navy
PoW	Prisoner of War
RHAW	Radar homing and warning system
RWR	Radar Warning Receiver
SA–7	ASCC codename for 9K32 Strela–2, Soviet MANPAD
SAC	Special Action Company
SAM	Surface–to–air missile
SAW	Squad Automatic Weapon
SRDP	Self–Reliance Development Program
SRB	Scout Ranger Battalion
SRC	Scout Ranger Company
SRR	Scout Ranger Regiment
SFB	Special Forces Battalion
SFC	Special Forces Company

SFR	Special Forces Regiment		USD	United States Dollar (also US$)
SW	Strike Wing		VHF	Very High Frequency
Sqn	Squadron		VIP	very important person
Sqn Ldr	Squadron Leader (military commissioned officer rank, equal to Major)		Wg Cdr	Wing Commander (military commissioned officer rank, equal to Lieutenant–Colonel)
TOG	Tactical Operations Group		WIA	Wounded in Action
USAF	United States Air Force		WWII	World War II

PREQUEL

During a visit in 2000 with my father to the United States Marine Corps museum in DC I purchased a book on the Philippine Marine Corps, much to my father's amusement. To a high school student in Northern Virginia this was an exotic subject which ended up spurring an interest in a civil war in a part of the world I knew little about and surprisingly little was written on in the last 20 years. I went out and purchased what books I could find in the English language on the Civil War in the Philippines. Six research trips to the Philippines have followed. and the seed of interest planted that afternoon has grown into this book.

For a nation best known in the USA for being a former colony and having exotic tourist locations, in only about 70 years of history since its independence, the Republic of the Philippines has seen an endless series of armed uprisings and civil wars that have killed over 100,000 individuals; insurgents, soldiers, and non–combatants. Indeed, the Philippines is in the unique and unfortunate situation of having to simultaneously face Islamist and Marxist insurgents.

The Philippines archipelago had been under Spanish domination since 16th Century then it fell under United States control after the war of 1898. The Philippine Nationalists were subdued after a bitter campaign though the country was eventually granted a semi–autonomous status in 1935, being run by the same class of political elite who had served the Spanish. Since 1946 the Philippines has been faced by Marxist insurgents, Islamist insurgents, ethnic separatist insurgents and disaffected elements of the military: presently, the government is facing insurgencies run by the New People's Army (NPA; Communist/Maoist by orientation), the Abu Sayyaf Group (ASG; extremist Islamists), the Bangamoro Islamic Freedom Fighters (BIFF; extremist Islamists), and has at times a tenuous cease fire with the Moro National Liberation Front (MNLF), and Moro Islamic Liberation Front (MILF). Corruption, human rights violations, ethnic strife, and a traditionally poor economy have fuelled wars that are raging on and off for close to 70 years.

There are many publications related to the issue of human rights in the Philippines. There are several publications about the Huk Revolt of the 1940s and 1950s, numerous books about the socio–political structure of insurgent movements and causes of numerous military revolts. More recently, some authors have discussed the emergence of the notorious Abu Sayyaf Group (ASG). However, there are few publications offering an overview of the military aspects of resulting conflicts. This prompted me to explore those areas.

Over the last 70 years, intensity of different conflicts has ranged from small unit fire fights to major battles between elite units of the Philippine armed forces and different insurgent groups, but sometimes reached proportions of large–scale, semi–conventional operations supported by artillery and armour. At least as important is the fact that all these wars are fought over entirely different parts of an archipelago with a coast line 36,289 km long and a total area of 300,000 km2 and including 7,107 of Islands, some of which are little more than a 'few rocks', while larger islands are comparable in size to Florida.

Correspondingly, primary purpose of this book is to track the general course of different civil wars in the Philippines, and provide a summary of combat operations by the Armed Forces of the Philippines (AFP), transformation of the military over this time in reaction to emergence of new threats. The coverage is therefore starting with the Huk Revolt of the 1940s, and early separatism of the Moros, to the revolt against the Marcos dictatorship. Final chapters are dedicated to the coverage of anti–terror operations against Islamist extremist insurgents since 11 September 2001, and other terror groups.

Because the situation on the battlefields of the Philippines has transformed from one of a clash between 'classic' popular uprisings and COIN campaigns run by conventional military into asymmetric warfare between militant groups and special forces supported by air force, in recent years, the secondary purpose of this book was to summarize this transformation.

Another characteristic of all these conflicts is that the Armed Forces of the Philippines (AFP) has been chronically – and, in recent times: 'increasingly' – underfunded. The AFP have to make do with obsolete weaponry not only when it comes to heavy equipment, but also in regards of small arms, light armoured vehicles and artillery. Facing increasing budget shortfalls, the military is meanwhile largely equipped with armament that is dating back to the Second World War and the Vietnam War. The classic example for this unusual situation is the Philippine Air Force (PhAF), which in recent years became entirely reliant on obsolescent light jets, converted training aircraft, elderly and worn–out helicopters, and other means to provide support for ground units. Correspondingly, the third purpose of this book is to describe various 'field–adaptations' of the armament as undertaken by the AFP, and to provide an introduction into covert and extra judicial operations taken to make up for short comings on the battlefield.

Facing such limitations, the government is increasingly reliant on local militias and 'covert means' for its counterinsurgency (COIN) operations. Shadowy extra judicial operations have been used hand in hand with traditional hearts and minds doctrine in an attempt to retake control of lost territory. This book is not intended to be a moral indictment of such methods, or those of the insurgents. Correspondingly, I'm purposely not discussing the morality of extra judicial killings, pseudo–terrorist operations, or torture, although these are related to much of developments in various conflicts on the Philippines. Similarly, space considerations have led to the exclusion of all disputes related to the Spratly Islands, much of the political and socio–economic history of the different movements, and recent raids of Moro insurgents into Malaysia.

With the end of the Cold War the international focus has shifted to the threat of international terrorism. The Southern Philippines became from the1990s onwards became a magnet for militants who were able to train and organize taking advantage of the fact considerable territory was outside of government control. With the widespread access to small arms even part time insurgents or bandits can boast considerable firepower. After the events of 11 September 2001 much attention was focused on the insurgency in the South.

CHAPTER 1
HUK REVOLT

Insurgent Forces

After independence, the nation was faced with a severe rural discontent over poverty and a corrupt and deeply entrenched political elite; creating an environment ripe for unrest. In the aftermath of the American liberation of the Philippines leftist activists were arrested by the government in an attempt to stem a revolt. The revolt began soon after independence in 1946. Seen as a communist insurrection from the beginning, although not actively supported by the Philippine Communist Party until 1950, the Hukbong Magpapalaya ng Bayan (Huk) in Tagalog acronym for People's Liberation Army had been among the most efficient Philippine guerrilla groups during the Second World War. Its cadres drew from peasant trade unions militants opposed the rural elites. After being banned from political life, the Huks, under the command of Luis Taruc, moved to the armed struggle. The insurgents developed a strong political organization with a supportive population allowing them to withstand government operations. By the year 1950 it was estimated that the Huks had around 15,000 fighters and 150,000 supporters. Philippine President Manuel Roxas launched a "mailed fist" approach attempting to break the revolt through military means, which failed. The first government response was an indiscriminate military campaign which succeeded only to push more peasants into the ranks of the Huks.

The Huks had a large infrastructure and widespread popular support in Central Luzon. Huk units were organized into squads, squadrons, battalions, field commands and finally regional commands. The insurgents had fought the Japanese and local collaborators for several years and were well versed in guerrilla warfare and had stocks of left over weapons. Their weapons were mainly left over equipment from Japan and America. Most of the weapons available to the Huks were light infantry weapons; the insurgents had no mortars larger then 81mm and no artillery. The Huks were politically divided into factions from hardcore communists, ex–guerrillas from the Second World War, disaffected peasants, and bandits. These were divided up between unarmed supporters, part time guerrillas, and full time guerrillas. Supporters would furnish information on government movements and provide supplies to the insurgents. The part time members conducted ambushes and also carried out administrative duties such as collecting supplies and relaying information while during the day operating as farmers.

Insurgents moved in small groups from six to twelve men, armed with light equipment, to prevent their discovery. Insurgent groups would combine to conduct raids or ambushes and then disperse again. With successful operations the Huks captured automatic weapons; soon some units had comparable firepower to PC units. Huk units also conducted extortion, including holding up buses and demanding bribes from passengers along with extorting villagers.

The insurgents were hampered by poor communications, units across Luzon were often cut off from regular communications with central headquarters. Radios were bought or captured but these were mainly used for intelligence. In the field, the Huks relied on messengers, beating tree trunks, shouting, firing tracers and animal calls. Groups would link up by following the direction of bent tree

Huk insurgents moving by river. With their weapons hidden they would raise little suspicion. (via Albert Grandolini)

APhAF L–5 dropping a 60mm mortar round on Huk positions. Along with FAC work some L–5 crews took to launching independent attacks on insurgent band with hand delivered mortar rounds and small incendiary bombs The damage inflicted was minimal but they had a nuisance value and kept insurgents off balance as heavier assets were brought to bear. (via Albert Grandolini)

F–51 being fitted loaded with 12.7mm machine gun rounds and bombs. Typically larger 500lb and 1000lb bombs were used by the F–51Ds on targets such as base camps and large formations only after FACs had identified them positively and the risk to civilian targets was lessened. The majority of airstrikes employed rockets, 100lb GP, 250lb Fragmentation and 300lb GP bombs in addition to the Browning machine guns calibre 12.7mm. Napalm tanks were also used by the end of the campaign, but their deployment required special authorization from the General Headquarters in each specific case. (via Albert Grandolini)

branches and other simple signs, meant to be unnoticed by casual observers. Civilian messengers were most commonly used for relaying information to the different bands of insurgents.

The Huks also took advantage of the poor system of unit demarcation, setting up near the points where sectors of responsibility intersected, relying on poor communications and coordination among the PC to allow their own units to operate freely. Strategically the movement focused most of its efforts in Central Luzon and Southern Tagalog, which enabled the numerically small PA/PC to deploy large forces to the area.

Origins of the Philippine Army and Constabulary

The centrepiece of the AFP, the Philippine Army (PA), traces its history to two military forces; the Philippine Scouts and Philippine Constabulary (PC). The PC was originally established on 8 August 1901 by the United States with the task of rural policing. It was a well trained and highly respected force, large parts of which became involved in a guerrilla war launched against Japanese occupation, in early 1942. Tragically, many of well-trained and skilled commanders and other ranks were killed during the following the Japanese occupation.

When the USA granted the Philippines independence on 4 July 1946, the only armed force really available for anti Huk operations was the Military Police Command (MPC), established with US support during the closing stages of the Second World War. Led by former Constabulary officers and veterans of insurgency against the Japanese occupation, the MPC was armed with little more but pistols and batons, and it took some time until all of its officers received carbines and rifles, followed by heavier infantry weapons (in turn, white

helmets and white jeeps it did have swiftly proved to be hopelessly out of their element when facing insurgents).

In 1948 the MPC was indissolved and elements were rebranded the as the Philippine Constabulary (PC). The mission of this force was internal security and it was initially under the control of the Secretary of the Interior. By 1948, the PC had increased to 12,000 officers and other ranks, and an additional 8,000 army soldiers were re-assigned to it for support, boosting it to around 20,000. In theory, the members of the PC underwent courses teaching them US Army's infantry tactics, but in practice this force was hurriedly deployed in the field while still short on experienced commanders and disciplined non-commissioned officers (NCOs). Indeed, because the government failed to establish itself even in control of much of the Luzon Island, before long the PC was entrusted even with the role of tax collection and were co-opted by provincial elites.

Meanwhile, the Philippine Army (PA) was re-established by the US for the planned invasion of Japan. By late 1945 there were 250,000 men under arms, a number which quickly dropped to 30,000 in the aftermath of the war. By the start of the Huk Revolt, the PA was a small service faced with leadership troubles, stemming from a large number of unqualified former reservists who ended up in command of combat units. The shortage of government troops coupled with the corrupt political system led to the rise of militias controlled by provincial elites. Through co-opting the police and through securing votes for national candidates, provincial elites were able to take control of the local police forces and waged mini-wars with insurgents and other political rivals.

A line of M–8 armoured cars. Small detachments of light–armoured vehicles were assigned to infantry battalions to support mobile operations. The main armament was a 37mm cannon, which could employ high explosive as well as canister rounds to great effect against ambushes. (via Albert Grandolini)

PA M116 75mm pack howitzer section side up on the side of a road to provide fire support. Plentiful use was made of artillery to shell suspected rebel concentrations during large scale sweeps. (via Albert Grandolini)

Private Initiative

The AFP was initially too small and scattered to suppress the insurgents. The PC and PA combined had around 37,000 personnel in the field. Each province received at least one PC company, with others receiving as many as 15. These companies would number around 100men each and were generally lightly equipped with small arms. Motor transport was limited and thus units could not move rapidly to respond to emergencies. After a series of initial clashes with the Huks the PC often remained inside fortified positions which allowed the insurgents to seize control of villages and towns. Making the situation worse was that captured Huks often had the right to bail, enabling some suspects to rejoin their units.

One of the few aggressive PC units was designated "Nenita", a unit which was marred by allegations of torture and extrajudicial killings. It was commanded by Major Napoleon Valeriano and supported by Edward Landsdale of the CIA. "Nenita" had a core of around 40–50 men, though it repeatedly drew reinforcements from other PC units, as necessary. "Nenita" developed into an elite strike force, tasked with in hunting down high value targets (HVTs) such as Luis Taruc. "Nenita" operated its own intelligence networks with some success, but failed in their mission of eliminating insurgent leadership. Typical operations were begun with "Nenita" cordoning off areas before launching aggressive sweeps. Often nearly every individual within the cordoned zone killed, regardless of his or her actual status. Unsurprisingly, such operations helped insurgent recruitment, and "Nenita" was eventually disbanded, although its officer cadre and most of personnel was

simply re–distributed to other units, and it became a model for other units of this kind.

Unlike "Nenita", most of other PC units preferred to remain their fortified bases, not venturing out into the countryside. In some cases, more aggressive commanders were hamstrung by local elites who demanded protection, and thus limited their activity to static defensive operations. PC major sweeps, rare and often ineffective, were often conducted because of local political pressure from land owners and businessmen. During these rare offensive operations the PC used tactics similar to those of the former Japanese occupying forces, the troops would loot and burn villages during major sweeps often out of anger over their inability to locate the elusive Huks. PC relations with the PhAF were generally good but initially due to administrative reasons there was no interagency arrangement between the services, making CAS dependent on local arrangements between units. Lacking money and supplies the PC was reported to have looted farms which only increased support for the Huks. Some 3,000 PC troopers were on operations against some 10,000 insurgents in Huklandia. The PC was further stretched by the need to suppress armed bandits on other islands.

Large scale sweeps of multiple battalions (often collections of multiple companies drawn from different battalions) remained the standard tactic with few insurgents being caught but much damage being inflicted on civilian farms and villages in the course. Observations by officers placed much of the failure of operations on lack of *reconnaissance* and poor patrolling techniques. Operations were largely road bound affairs, ending before dark to avoid rebel ambushes. Large scale actions while often clumsily were far from useless, producing steady losses in men and equipment to the Huks.

Force X

Throughout 1948, the Huks stepped up raids and ambushes. Large scale offensives conducted with much press coverage failed to achieve lasting results. Despite killing Huk members the AFP was unsuccessful in capturing or killing Huk leadership, promoting the Constabulary to form another elite unit tasked with eliminating HVTs. This unit came to be known as "Force–X" a unit of 47 men drawn from the 116th Constabulary Company and tasked with pseudo guerrilla operations. This unit was organized similar to a comparable Huk unit, with similar weapons, uniforms and nicknames and members even learned the mannerisms of the guerrillas through interrogation of captured Huk members.[1] The mission of this unit was to infiltrate the Huk movement and gather intelligence and conduct direct action

---

1   Weapons were altered to show signs of poor maintenance and abuse so as to not appear too well equipped.

Armed T–6s served alongside the F–51Ds providing CAS for ground forces. Armed T–6s were a common fixture of post–WW–2 COIN operations and saw service as in Latin America, Algeria and Indochina. (via Albert Grandolini)

A well armed force of Huk insurgents in 1950. These men are armed with standard AFP issue small arms including two Browning Automatic Rifles (BAR). These weapons would have been captured from government forces in raids and ambushes. (via Albert Grandolini)

PA troops conducting a sweep. The soldiers wear American style uniforms and are armed with a mix of M–1 Garands, M–1 Carbines and a BAR. With the advantage of motorization and with excellent communications with the PhAF and artillery units, AFP ground troops could move lightly encumbered with small arms, ammunition light rations, water during sort range patrols. (via Albert Grandolini)

missions against the Huks. Force X had to create its own intelligence networks among the civilian population. Careful *reconnaissance* of Huk territory was conducted before operations and mock battles with the PA and PC were often conducted to provide a cover for Force–X. The weakness of Huk communications and command and control allowed Force–X to infiltrate the insurgents. In their first operation lasting almost a week, Force–X joined a camp with the 7th and 15th Huk Squadrons without raising serious suspicions among the insurgents. Additional insurgents entered the camps, comprising the 4th and 21st Squadrons. Force–X sprung a nocturnal ambush killing 82 Huks outright, with another 21 Huks being killed and 26 captured in a follow up army sweep.

While this unit was able to reap huge successes relative to its size, and led to the Huk units sometimes engaging each other out of the fear that the other was possibly Force–X, it was too limited in size to really have a major effect on the course of the war. By the time the unit was disbanded it had helped destroy four squadrons of Huk insurgents.

New President Elpidio Quirino took a softer line with the insurgents, hoping that peace talks would succeed. Amnesty was offered in the summer of 1948 but the program fell apart as Huk defectors were abused by the AFP and the Huk leadership used the time to reorganize. The breakdown of the talks led to the government taking a harder line with the insurgents.

In April 1949, a massive operation was conducted as a response to the murder, by Huk insurgents, of the widow and the daughter of former Philippine President Manuel Quezon. The murder itself was a major political blunder and created a groundswell of public indignation against the Huks. The AFP launched a major operation with two PC battalions, one Army Infantry Battalion, an armoured *reconnaissance* company and battery of field artillery. The operation was surprisingly effective, the 4,000 man force, moving in company sized columns spreadheaded by small unit patrols, were able to kill over 100 insurgents and capture another 40 over the next several months. Despite the insurgents knowing of the attacks they were also hampered by the terrain and poor communications and were unable to mass forces or determine the units' intentions. The AFP used aggressive interrogations of captured insurgents to conduct follow on

PA troops moving through a town.
(via Albert Grandolini)

M8 and M20 armoured cars on patrol.
(via Albert Grandolini)

raids which allowed the AFP to capture or kill the entire unit behind the attack on the former First Lady.

Establishment of the Philippine Air Force

In September 1945, the PAAC received its first Stinson L–5 Sentinel liaison aircraft from the USA. This was followed by two Douglas C–47 Dakota transports, which entered service with the 1st Troop Carrier Squadron. Following the independence, the Philippines began receiving increasing amounts of US aid, and by January 1946 a total of 22 C–47s were delivered, although not all of these became operational – this time because of lack of qualified personnel. Next to be formed was the 1st Air Squadron equipped with Piper L–4 Grasshopper

liaison planes, in March 1946. This was augmented with additional L–5s and then reorganized as the 1st Liaison Squadron.

The PhAF activated its first combat squadron, the 1st Fighter Squadron, on 1 May 1946. Although the USA supplied a batch of F–51Ds as soon as June 1946, they had been held on storage at Clark Air Force Base. Very little flying was actually carried out unit until well into 1947. The pilots sometimes got to assist in the training role of the 1st Liaison Squadron or borrow an L–5. Meanwhile, a second fighter unit, the 2nd Fighter Squadron was activated by early 1947, but remained very much a "paper" unit, that appears never to had even a commanding officer appointed.

The lack of personnel, logistic support and technical infrastructures considerably slowed down the establishment of the PhAF fighter force

PA ground troops. Unarmoured trucks remain today the primary way to move troops around the warzone despite the risk of mines and ambush. (via Albert Grandolini)

PA troops on patrol. (via Albert Grandolini)

though organizational works continued. It was decided to rename the two fighter squadrons as being the 6th and 7th Fighter Squadrons. The number "6" was chosen to commemorate the pre–war 6th Pursuit Squadron. To complete the organizational change, the 5th Fighter Group was created on 1 November 1947 at Basa Air Base.

The first batch of Mustangs finally entered service on 24 October 1947. Eighteen were initially placed into service with the remainder fifteen held in storage. The PhAF fighter force was still in its infancy and for the first couple of years all the fighter pilots were veterans of the pre–war PAAC. Training was haphazard and there were no permanent US instructors at Basa. Maintenance was also poor with very basic technical facilities, resulted in an operational rate with 25percent for the F–51Ds. Lack of flying discipline and experience also led to several crashes. Several aircraft were lost when their pilots performed low level aerobatic for their friends and relatives over their houses and even over Manila University. Nevertheless, the F–51s arrived in the nick of time as the internal tensions had degenerated into a vicious civil war.

In the meantime, on 1 October 1947 under Executive Order 94 the newly renamed Philippine Air Force (PhAF) became an official branch of the Armed Forces of the Philippines. In exchange for granting basing rights for a period of 99 years to the US military, the Philippines subsequently received additional surplus military aircraft. The US military established a number of major facilities in the Philippines, including the Clark Field AB (Central Luzon), Subic Bay (Olongapo Harbour), and Naval Air Station Cubi Point.

Changing the Course

President Quirino was forced to take a hard line with the Huks. The government appointed Ramon Magsaysay, a former Second World War guerrilla leader who had gone into politics, as Defense Minister who was helped by US advisers of the Joint United States Military Advisory Group (JMAG). The nascent CIA also supported the effort under the supervision of Colonel Lansdale. The new campaign encompassed military, political and social approaches.

This effort came at the right moment, because in March 1950 the Huks started a large offensive against San Mateo, San Simon, Los

Motorized patrol resting. (via Albert Grandolini)

To strike the insurgents a C–47 was also modified to be used as a bomber. Dubbed the XBC–47, the aircraft had six external pylons under the fuselage, between the main landing gears, that allowed it to carry light fragmentation bombs. (via Albert Grandolini)

M116 pack howitzer crew conducting a fire mission. (via Albert Grandolini)

Banos and Montalban, in the hopes that government troops would be surprised and quickly overpowered. In August there was a second attack by the Huks, who had renamed their armed wing the People's Liberation Army (PLA). Magsaysay took rapid steps to improve both the Army and Constabulary. The defence budget was tripled. Senior officers accused of corruption were fired; officers who performed well were promoted as Magsaysay attempted to create a professional sprit into the military. Magsaysay increased the pay of enlisted personnel to prevent the need to forage for food which alienated civilians and to improve morale among soldiers. The major target of the campaign shifted from the Huks on the field to the hearts and minds of the local population and Magsaysay took steps to improve military and police discipline to prevent abuses of the population. The government set up a telegram system to allow civilians to provide intelligence and complain of abuses by government troops. For a major operation to be approved it needed to have three objectives; to gain civilian cooperation, to gain intelligence, and to kill or capture Huks.

Of critical importance was the formation of the Battalion Combat Teams (BCT). The BCT was made up of a headquarters company, three rifle companies of around 110 men each, a fire support company, a *reconnaissance* company with armoured cars and dismounts, and often operated with a battery of light artillery attached. This organization provided both the flexibility to conduct small unit patrols over large areas and the fire power to conduct major sweeping operations. The 1,100 men BCT was to become the standard unit of operation in the Army for the remainder of the conflict. From the first one, the 7th BCT in 1950, their number grew to some 26 within four years. The new units relied more on non conventional tactics, emphasizing secrecy, intelligence and psychological warfare, and reduced the random brutality against the civilian population. Cameras were provided to patrols, to photograph rebel corpses to provide proof of claimed rebel losses. The PC was reduced in strength to 7,600 men, as men were transferred to the PA, and on 23 December 1950 was transferred to the Department of National Defense.

The newly (re)formed Philippine Navy (PN) established a Marine Company which was initially assigned to a PA BCT for COIN operations. The Marines, using fishing boats and small PN boats, conducted a series of small unit amphibious landings in support of major operations. The BCTs operated often nearly autonomously under Brigade sized sector commands. The PN itself was a small service relying on ex–USN coastal minesweepers and PC–461 and SC–497 class submarine chasers supported by various light patrol boats.

The officer cadre had to be reformed to groom officers who could aggressively take the war to the guerrillas and work with local political elites and the rural population to conduct a hearts and minds campaign. BCTs were typically broken up as companies and platoons were assigned to towns and villages. Movement was conducted by trucks and patrolling done on foot. Convoys ambushed by insurgents were trained to respond quickly, undamaged vehicles were to escape from the kill zone and drop off infantry who would assault the flanks of the insurgents, where the front and rear vehicles blocked the roads units were trained to attack the ambush frontally.

From 1950, Magsayay attempted to solve to the Huk Revolt at its roots and established various hearts and minds programs. Captured and surrendered Huks were brought back into society and many were given land on other islands to set up farms. In later years the movement of landless peasants from Luzon would create tensions in Mindanao, where most were sent. In the short term these programs drastically undercut support for the Huks and caused over one thousand members to rally to the government. Civilian militias, managed by local political elites, were set up in areas the Huks raided to allow villagers to better protect themselves, which freed up army and Constabulary units from static defence. These private militias in some areas acted as private armies for the political elites but did linit insurgent activity through both defensive operations and through extrajudicial methods.

The BCTs were reinforced and became the source of increased American attention. Eventually much of the heavy equipment was removed from the units, leaving only 81mm mortars and recoilless rifles, and the former weapons crews fought as light infantry to better cover large distances. From 1950 there was an increase in Special

The L–5 took part in duties as varied as FAC, transportation, and psychological operations (PSYOPS), showing itself to be probably the PhAF's most versatile platform. (via Albert Grandolini)

Operations Forces (SOF). A plan to create an airborne unit for the Philippine Army was begun with a company, later expanded into a full battalion by 1951, being trained but never employed in the airborne role. The Scout Rangers, combining the legacy of the Alamo Scouts and US Army Rangers, were formed to conduct long range *reconnaissance* patrols. Originally these were five man teams, consisting of one officer and four enlisted men, attached to each BCT but in time they were formed into a unit of their own, the Scout Ranger Regiment (SRR). Scout Rangers specialized in long duration patrols lasting often a week at a time. Around 7,700 Scout Rangers were trained by the end of the war making them the largest SOF unit in the military.

Regular infantry units conducted similar operations, from conducting small unit raids against HVTs to operating in a style as Force–X and conducting pseudo terrorist operations. The AFP infiltrated men into the Huk movements, supplied with money and weapons, and used them to map the inner workings of the organization determining the names and locations of insurgent leadership. AFP raids acting on this intelligence would then kill or capture HVTs and helped break the financial and logistics organization.

Air Force at War in the 1950s

The PhAF involvement in the campaign was initially limited to observation and transport missions. The lack of transport assets also pushed the government to contract civilian DC–3s to fly troops and supplies. In conjunction with its training activities, the 5th FG got involved in the escalating operations against the Huks too. Some enterprising and aggressive pilots began to attack insurgents from L–4 or L–5 aircraft with hand grenades and mortar shells. Some T–6 trainers were also armed with machine guns and light bombs and used in ground attack missions.

During 1950 the AFP succeeded in pushing the Huks out of heavily populated areas, which in turn gave the PhAF a freer hand to conduct attack missions. After the Korean War broke out the US increased the flow of aid to the AFP. Fifty additional F–51s were delivered in 1950, followed by 40 in 1953, 2 in 1954 and finally 24 in 1955. The

Mechanized PA unit mounted in M–3 Scout Cars on a routine patrol. The vehicles carried a 12.7mm M–2 Heavy Machinegun and two M–1919 Medium Machineguns along with a small infantry section. (via Albert Grandolini)

additional airframes allowed the set up of the 8th Fighter Squadron 1951. Several F–51s were hit by small arms fire, though none were lost to enemy action. The fighter squadrons were based near Manila, but detachments of F–51s were spread out throughout Luzon.

An armoured unit made up of M–8 Armoured Cars conducting a patrol. (via Albert Grandolini)

M–3 Scout Car displaying four machine guns, giving it formidable counter–ambush firepower. (via Albert Grandolini)

PA soldiers on patrol. With the advantage of training and the ability to call in heavy firepower PA/PC ground troops aggressively took the war to the insurgents. (via Albert Grandolini)

Maintenance was still poor due to a shortage of spare parts, trained ground crews and the rough local conditions; thirty pilots died in accidents. Initially the majority of air strikes conducted were against area targets and there was poor coordination between the PhAF and PA/PC and thus F–51s were called to strike area targets in the hopes of killing insurgents. The Mustangs often flew missions lasting up to four hours long to patrol the northern coast of Luzon, trying to intercept suspecting boats believed to be bringing supplies to the insurgents. None were ever spotted.

During the conflict the PhAF flew around 2,600 CAS missions. The planes used for the vast majority of the ground attack sorties were the F–51Ds followed by the T–6 trainers. Operation Four Roses in April 1952 was an example of the new tactics as F–51s conducted 68 strike missions against Huk camps in the Sierra Madre Mountains based on

intelligence from ground forces and L–5s acting as FACs. By 1952 on, the PhAF deployed an average of two L–5s on forward airfields to act as FACs for the F–51s. PhAF pilots were assigned to BCTs to provide liaison services and coordinate air operations.

<cap> 0116

The L–5 was the true workhorse of the PhAF. Long duration operations BCTs could last for weeks and patrols were reliant on daily air drops from L–5s. In a major test two BCTs were supported by two L–5s which over a month long operation dropped supplies to the ground forces. The pilots had to learn to take measures to disguise the position of patrols they were supporting. This came in the form of dummy drops of supplies and changing flight paths.

L–5s were also used to hidden locate farms used by the Huks to feed their forces. Once the farms were found they would be attacked from the air or ground troops would be launch a sweep in the hopes of cutting off food to the guerrillas. The Huks would hide at the sight of an L–5 knowing it could either be on a *reconnaissance* mission or carrying small bombs of its own. L–5s also conducted special operations; several were fitted with loud speakers and would travel over Huk territory and thank members by name for providing information to the government along with dropping flyers offering amnesty to Huk members. The PhAF also used captured guerrillas to speak into loud speakers from airplanes calling on their comrades to surrender. The use of helicopters in this conflict was however limited as only a few light Bell 47 helicopters were in government service. Yet these helicopters conducted vital medical evacuation missions.

Breaking the Revolt

The reformed AFP took to the field against a rebel movement which was launching attacks across Luzon. The Huks raided Camp Macabulos located in Tarlac Province during 1950. The army suffered 20 casualities and the insurgents made off with weapons, ammunition and other supplies. Other raids were conducted in Luzon against government positions. In Palauig, in 1951 around 100 insurgents attacked the town from four directions. They burned down houses and the municipal building before reinforcements could arrive. The slow response was a mark of the poor infrastructure and the inability to move troops quickly, road transport was the fastest way to respond.

The AFP conducted ruthless covert and extra–judicial operations, targeting high level supporters and agents of the Huks. Through bribes and torture rebel leadership was discovered and the leaders

A PhAF PBY–5A flying boat operating as part of SATAG. These planes were heavily employed as maritime patrol planes and for search and rescue operations. (via Albert Grandolini)

were killed or arrested. The Military Intelligence Service (MIS) used former Huk insurgents in a campaign to kill insurgent leadership on Pasay Island. On 16 September 1951 the Panay Task Force launched Operation Mouse Trap, setting up a cordon ringing several towns. Inside the cordon was believed to be the leading the Panay Huks. Two days later Scout Ranger teams arrived and conducted raids in the area and took prisoners and questioned the locals and built on their success, conducting further raids based on intelligence gained from operations.[2]

The guerrilla suffered a major setback in September 1952 with Operation Knockout which saw the fall of the Huk bastion in the Visaya Province and the elimination of one of its best commanders, Guillermo Capadocia.[3] The AFP's gradual dismantlement of the Huk politico–administrative infrastructures led the guerrillas to lose the protection and support of local peasants.

By the start of 1954 the Huks were a broken force both militarily and politically. Much of their popular support had eroded and on the battlefield aggressive patrols and new tactics allowed the government to reduce the movement to less than 2,000 members. Huk farms were destroyed which in turn forced them to raid civilian farms, turning them into bandits in the eyes of many peasants. The loss of food supplies further broke rebel morale and bands of exhausted insurgents surrendered en–masse. The number of fighters had also been reduced to around 2,000.

From February to mid–September of 1954 the AFP launched the largest anti–Huk offensive of the war, Operation Thunder–Lightning which resulted in the surrender of Luis Taruc, chairman of the organization's Military Committee. Further clean–up operations of guerrillas remaining lasted throughout 1955, diminishing its number to less than one thousand by year's end. Between 1950 and 1955 over 6,000 insurgents were killed, almost 5,000 captured and around 2,000 wounded. What clinched victory were a flexible political leadership, the professionalism of the AFP, the ability to keep pressure on the insurgents and the fact the rebellion mostly took place on Central Luzon allowing the AFP to mass troops.

Moslem Revolt

While the government seemed to be overcoming the communist insurrection, another trouble spot developed in Mindanao in 1954. A Moslem uprising flared up, led by Hadji Kamlon, another former anti–Japanese guerrilla leader, who resented, among others, the grant of land to Huk defectors and enterprising Christians.

The Marines were deployed to engage the insurgents. The Marine company fought at the platoon and squad level against Kamlon. The fighting went on as Marines and Kamlon conducted small scale

2 The Scout Rangers were divided into four groups made up of three teams.
3 Employing the 7th, 16th, 17th, and 22nd BCTs.

PA mechanized patrol mounted in an M–3 Scout Car. Such vehicles were able to keep the roads secure, escort convoys and assist in large scale operations. The vehicle's mobility would–be seriously limited were it to try and manoeuvre off the road. (via Albert Grandolini)

A T–33 of the 5th FW, soon these planes would be conducting CAS operations against insurgents with their 12.7mm machineguns and unguided ordinance. (via Albert Grandolini)

amphibious raids against each other. The PN conducted patrols with small boats and provided fire support for small scale landings by ground forces. Three PC companies were assigned to Cotabato. These companies were so under–strength that at any given time as few as 15 men were on duty. These units were assigned to important towns, limiting the available manpower for patrolling.

On 4 January 1955 bandits struck Kibugtongan, robbing homes, kidnapping civilians and destroying the bridge at Motain. The next day a small detachment of the PC moved by truck to find the bandits, slogging slowly over the muddy roads. They clashed at the Mulita Bridge as the bandits caught sight of a patrol moving on foot towards the bridge and fired wildly through the rain. One rebel died in the follow up, two days later 12 surrendered. These Moro revolts were small scale affairs, often compared at the time to banditry as they lacked a unified leader and were not of such a tempo to force major redeployments. The insurgents relied on what weapons they could find and were poorly trained. The government response was punitive campaigns and reacting to insurgent attacks. Eventually 5,000 government troops were in action against a several hundred–man insurgent force.

The PhAF reacted by setting up the Sulu Air Task Group (SATAG) to support Army operations against the insurgents. The task ground was made up of elements of the 6th and 7th Fighter Squadrons and boasted over 23 pilots and 73 airmen, eight F–51s, four Catalina PBY–5As and four L–5s and was later supplied with two H–19 helicopters. In addition to give close air support to the Army, the Mustangs also patrolled the sea lines around Mindanao to cut off supply lines to the

With the exception of the events of 1989 the F–5As of the 5th FW were destined to spend their career providing support for ground troops. The fleet, once the pride of the PhAF, would linger in its last decades as age and lack of funding caught up with them. (via Albert Grandolini)

Between 1958 and 1959 thirty–six T–34As were supplied to the PhAF. In the 1970s to make up for the short fall in ground attack assets they were used on combat operations. Several T–34s were assigned to the 15th Strike Wing as a stop gap until the T–28Ds and SF–260WPs entered service. (via Albert Grandolini)

The HU–16 had a very active career with the PhAF conducting not only search and rescue but also undertaking maritime patrol, ground attack, and even FAC duties. (via Albert Grandolini)

M–8 and M–20 armoured cars. Such vehicles, while primarily road bound, were of great use in convoy escorts and patrols. (via Albert Grandolini)

insurgents. From May 1955, the PhAF was given permission to strike suspected insurgent targets without prior authorization from ground forces. Colonel Benito Ebuen, then Commander of the PhAF, took part in the campaign for a while. The fighting went on for two years as the Marines and Kamlon conducted amphibious raids against each other. The L–5s proved once more time vital in this conflict again as FACs and conducting special psyops against the Muslim insurgents. The SATAG was disbanded in October 1955. Kamlon surrendered after two years. A combination of airpower and amphibious operations broke the back of the rebellion as the commanders surrendered and were jailed by the government.

CHAPTER 2
ARMING FOR THE WRONG WAR

By the year 1956, what was left of the communist insurgency had been all but defeated. Few scattered groups remained active in the countryside, foremost in Tarlac Province, but their activity was limited to low–intensity banditry, and the task of confronting them was taken over by the PC. With the Huks all but defeated, the AFP sought ways to reorganize and modernize. Reverting to a more conventional mindset and in cooperation with the USA, the military began preparing to wage a conventional conflict. The Army was decreased in size, while the PhAF was to be re–designed for defence from external threats, foremost from the People's Republic of China.

PhAF Golden Age

To bolster training needs an additional 38 T–6 trainers were supplied from 1956. The helicopter fleet was also expanded when five more Sikorsky S–55s had arrived the same year, bringing the fleet to ten, which in 1969 were augmented by three Sikorsky S–58s. The days of the piston–engine F–51s were ending despite the fact the 5th Fighter Wing had put 74 Mustangs in the air for the Independence Day fly-past of 1956.

The first jet aircraft supplied to the PhAF was the Lockheed T–33 which were delivered in August 1955. Four PhAF pilots had been previously trained as instructors on the type in Japan. The PhAF received a first batch of 24 T–33s that were grouped within 105th Combat Crew Training Squadron of the 5th Fighter Wing (5th FW) as the former 5th Fighter Group had been renamed. The first true jet fighter to enter service was the North American F–86F fighter bomber, which was supplied in 1957. The first 30 Sabres entered service with 5th FW replacing the older piston engine F–51Ds. Initially it was planned to keep the F–51Ds in service as advanced trainers, but an accident in June 1959 caused the PhAF to decide to replace them. By early 1960s the PhAF could deploy a force of sixty F–86Fs. The 8th FS was the last to retain its Mustangs when it was also converting to the all weather F–86D. The unit was declared operational in 1960 with 24 F–86Ds on strength. The new all jet force was more suited in countering the perceived threat from Communist Chinese then to support COIN operations. Meanwhile, in 1962 the 9th TFS "Limbas" was formed to respond to a request from the UN for support for the operations in the Congo. Personnel for the unit were drawn from the 5th Fighter Wing. The unit served a four–month deployment, flying air support missions for UN ground forces on Italian supplied F–86Es.

In October 1965 the 5th FW was reinforced with the arrival of the first Northrop F–5A/B fighters, which were supersonic and had the ability to carry AIM–9B air–to–air missiles. Some 22 F–5As and eight F–5Bs were received in the next two years. They reequipped the 6th FS which had relinquished its remaining F–86Fs to the 7th FS, the 8th FS when it retired its F–86Ds in July 1968, and the 9th FS.

A force of MNLF insurgents with Libyan supplied FN–FALs in addition to captured M–16A1s, M–14s, M–1 Garands, an M–1 Carbine and an M–1919 machine gun. Thanks to Libyan support small groups of NLF insurgents were often as well armed as comparably sized government units. (via Albert Grandolini)

The first 12 North American T–28As arrived in the country in 1959, with 20 in service by 1960 with the 102nd Pilot School Squadron. In the year prior, Beechcraft T–34 Mentors had been supplied by Japan as part of war reparations. Both planes were capable of being armed but were used as trainers. After serving with the 101st Pilot School, the Mentors were handed over in 1968 to the Reserve Airlift and Tactical Support Service (RATSS), an auxiliary air force which acted as a reserve component of the PhAF. They were replaced by 28 Cessna T–41Ds while the T–28As were supplemented by 27 SIAI SF–260MPs from August 1967. Importantly for future needs were the O–1/L–19s, and L–4/L–5s which arrived throughout the decade. Several of each was received in the early 1960s, and more throughout the decade. The planes would later serve as forward air controllers, liaison duties and for scout work. The old C–47s were heavily tasked and additional airframes were acquired. They were supported in the transport role from 1959 on with the delivery of the firsts of the 13 Fokker F 27s and some DHC–3 Otters. In August 1957 the first of 13 Grumman HU–16 Albatross amphibians [4] were delivered and were based at Sangley Point Airbase and operated by the 505th Air Rescue Squadron.

The service as a whole was maintained with heavy American assistance and become one of the most modern South East Asian air forces for the Philippines were acted as the main rear base for the US operations in Vietnam. The PhAF had a good mission ready rate and the pilots were well trained to fight a large scale conventional war. But even if the PhAF now had a considerable number of highly competent

---

4 The first four were actually SA–16As and the remaining nine were a mix of HU–16B/D/Es.

NPA insurgents. (via Albert Grandolini)

PA M41 Walker–Bulldog light tanks on parade. (via Albert Grandolini)

NPA rebels with a mix of M–16s and AK–47s. (via Albert Grandolini)

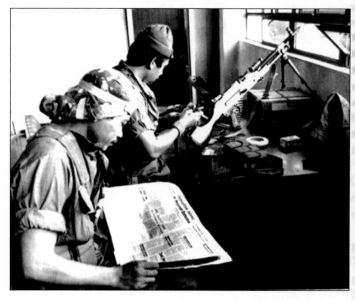

PA soldiers with a non–standard FN–MAG. (via Albert Grandolini)

personnel, sometimes hired by the CIA for clandestine operations throughout Asia, it was clear that without the US "logistical tail", the country could not afford such an air force.

Special Warfare Capability

During the 1960s, the Philippine political elite favoured the PC – which had the role of ensuring law and order in the cities and the countryside, which made it politically useful – and therefore this continued receiving the best manpower and much of funding. By the late 1960s the PC was receiving seven million dollars in American aid. The PC was essentially a military organization called upon to handle civil law enforcement missions. PC battalions were dispersed among the PC Zones. Small detachments of the PC were deployed all over the country, some facing the remaining Huks, various other local bands, and Moro bandits. During the decade clashes between Moros and Catholic settlers grew in frequency. The Huks had devolved into a criminal enterprise and clashed with the PC during bank robberies and other illegal activities. Clashes with the insurgents were small scale with the Huks avoiding clashes with the AFP. The PC had an active system of informants in the insurgents.

President Ferdinand Marcos began to expand his control by strengthening the PC and seizing control of provincial law enforcement. The army was deployed only in large scale punitive actions against bandit groups. Units of the PC took on a Special Forces role with airborne qualified A–Teams being deployed around the country, with one Special Forces company in the Capital and the remaining four being deployed to support other Constabulary commands. Yet within two years the unit was disbanded after becoming involved in local politics. The other elite unit of the Constabulary was the Rangers, elite light infantry tasked with counter insurgency operations. The special

warfare capability of the regular army was reorganized with the help from the USA. In 1958 a team of US Army Special Forces – popularly called 'Green Berets' – were deployed to the Philippines to conduct training with the PA. The first Philippine Special Forces team was activated in 1961 and in 1962 the first company of 107 officers and men was formed. The unit was modelled on the US Special Forces, where a 12 man A–Team made up of members who were cross trained with different skills; these were then grouped into B–Teams under the command of a major. Training involved parachuting, patrolling, *reconnaissance*, civil affairs and heavy weapons training. Within two years this new company was tasked with operations against Moro bandits in Sulu.

The Philippine Navy, organized, trained and equipped as a small coastal patrol force, lagged behind other branches of the AFP. It was equipped with two WW–2 vintage Destroyer Escorts, around a dozen Auk and Admirable class minesweepers employed as patrol corvettes, seven PGM–39 patrol boats, two Landing Ship Tank (LST), and three Landing Ship Mediums (LSM) left over from the Second World War. Maritime patrol support was provided by four Grumman HU–16B amphibian aircraft (which entered service already in 1955), but the PhAF was generally not equipped for overwater operations: its last two remaining PBY–5As (out of four delivered) were retired in 1959.[5] The Marine Corps continued to slowly expand, adding an additional rifle company, a fire support company, engineers, a Scout Raider Platoon. Its units took part in small punitive campaigns against bandits and remaining Huk bands which had devolved into rural bandits.

---

5   . One had earlier sunk after a rough water landing and another had struck debris on the surface of water and sank.

Despite the facade, the Philippines remained economically weak and over–dependent on the United States. The AFP thus was capable of limited counter insurgency operations and patrolling coastal waters, there was criticism in the press that the AFP lacked the ability to fight a major conflict for more than a brief period.

Operation Merkada

Externally, the Philippines had a dispute with the newly formed Federation of Malaysia. In 1962 the Philippines claimed the Sabah province of northern Malaysia as part of the historical Sultanate of Sulu. British tradition of paying a "rent" to the Sultan was used as an excuse for legitimating this claim, despite the Sultanate being long since out of power and despite subsequent agreements between the US and UK to delineate the borders and a UN commission. The US and UK effectively sided with Malaysia over the matter much to the anger of nationalistic press in the Philippines. The situation was made embarrassing for the Philippine Government when the RAF used Clark AFB to refuel six Hunter fighter jets bound for the Sabah. Following a few standoffs and shows of force near the disputed border, talks broke down., The PhAF deployed a C–47 to conduct patrols inside Malaysian waters and deployed patrol boats off the Sabah coast. The Royal Navy conducted patrols in the disputed water alongside Malaysian patrol boats. During the sabre rattling the UK stated it would support Malaysia if Malaysia were attacked, leading to the residence of the British being burned by a nationalist mob.

President Marcos ordered the AFP to prepare plans to seize this province, despite knowing the US would not support such an attack. The centrepiece of this plan, Operation Merkada, was to become a group of about 100 Moro commandos trained by the Philippine Special Forces at Corregidor Island. They were planned to launch a series of commando operations, sabotages and demolitions aiming to destabilizing the authority of Malaysian Government in the Sabah.

NPA rebels conducting propaganda broadcasts. (via Albert Grandolini)

Seventeen agents had been infiltrated into Sabah by the AFP to support the raiders. The plot collapsed when the Moros, who had been under–paid and abused by their trainers, were informed about their mission: they refused and some 26 were killed in the subsequent exchange of fire with Special Forces. One of commandos survived, however, and escaped from Corregidor, subsequently informing the media. When the news broke of this so–called Jabidah Massacre – there followed a nationwide scandal. The political opposition believed this plot was part of a plan to form a strike force targeting political rivals. President Marcos denied all allegations and instead blamed "rogue elements" within the Special Forces of conducting this operation without his knowledge. As a result, the Special Forces were re–named as the Home Defence Forces Group (HDFG), and reduced to two companies but this made little difference – whether for the Philippine public, the shocked Moros, or the very worried Malayan authorities.

CHAPTER 3
COMMUNIST AND MORO UPRISINGS

With ethnic and religious tensions raising not only in the public but in armed forces during the 1960s, the Southern Philippines remained a powder keg. In 1967 an obscure student activist known as Nur Misuari founded the Muslim Nationalist League. The basic issues of social inequity and uneven development raised by the dissidents remained largely unresolved despite a weak land reform initiative. This led to the rise of long running separatist movement.

The first major movement was led by the Moro National Liberation Front (MNLF) which sparked a revolt among the Moslems living in the Sulu Archipelago and the Mindanao Island in 1968. The Government initially dispatched the 1st Company of Special Forces (Airborne), trained specially by the US advisers, to support local PC and PA units in quelling the uprising. Soon two Special Forces teams, ten PC companies and two entire PA BCTs were in action on Cotabato. The situation seemed to be settle down until the violence erupted again four years later. The MNLF had in meantime developed its logistical infrastructures and recruited troops with the help of foreign governments.

Still worried about a possible Philippine invasion, Malaysia began to work out its own plan to support an insurgency. The local Sabahan provincial government allowed Libya, to provide weapons and training to Moro insurgents. Libya's involvement was for political and "moral" reasons, the regime sought to export its style of revolution to other nations around the world. The Libyan leader was also angered by reports of massacres against Muslim civilians. Malaysia was not a revolutionary state but in effect turned a blind eye to Libyan support, to allow it to weaken the Philippines.

New People's Army

To deal with the Marxist insurgents on Luzon Task Force Lawin was set up with eventually 5,000 troops to operate in Central Luzon. On 29 March 1969, anniversary date when the guerrilla resistance against the Japanese was set up, the Communist Part of the Philippines (CPP) proclaimed the establishment of the New People's Army (NPA). The new communist party looked to the Maoist model of a long term guerrilla war, hoping to gradually build up local support and a strong base and only then to move to overthrow the government through direct military action. Units would target villages for infiltration, conduct raids and assassinations of local political elites, and eventually create shadow governments in communist controlled areas. Supported by China, this small group of less than 100 insurgents with hardly any weapons quickly gained in strength, prompting the AFP to went into

The aftermath of a successful ambush by MNLF insurgents. In guerrilla ambushes and raids the MNLF was highly successful but they were too lightly equipped for positional fighting. (via Albert Grandolini)

A DHC–2 being armed with 250lb bombs. The DHC–2 was actively converted into a ground attack plane; sixteen were fitted with 12.7mm machineguns and 70mm rocket pods, three were armed with 12.7mm machine guns and one with 30 calibre machine guns. There was criticism in some quarters of the US government because some of the planes had been supplied for a low price for use in developmental projects and were armed in violation of the agreement. (via Albert Grandolini)

action. Because of aggressive military operations in Tarlac Province, the NPA was forced to break into small groups and escape. However, in their escape the insurgents left behind incriminating records, including detailed operational plans and membership lists.

One of the first communist targets was the Philippine Air Force and the airplanes of different airlines. On 8 March 1968 an Fokker F–27 of the Air Manila was sabotaged and the plane crashed on Panay Island, with 18 passengers and crewmembers dying. On 21 April 1970 a similar incident occurred on a Hawker Siddeley HS–748 of the Philippines Air Lines (PAL) and six weeks later a bomb exploded on board an F–27 of the same company.

The RT–33A was assigned to the 105th CCTS of the 5th FW alongside armed T–33s. (via Albert Grandolini)

Nevertheless, the NPA continued growing and was soon receiving a steady intake of recruits like former Huk insurgents and college radicals, growing to about 800 combatants armed with rifles, pistols, and home–made shot–guns, by 1970. Facing them were over 7,000 troops drawn from combat units of the PC and the Army, of which the former bore the brunt of the fighting. It was under these circumstances that this once small insurgent movement formed the basis for one of major threats to the Philippine Government.

In the spring and summer of 1970 in Pampanga soldiers of the 10th and 20th IBs with the PC 51st battalion launched a series of raids which captured several HVTs and rank and file members, overran several camps. Captured insurgents were sometimes flown on PhAF U–17s to secure prisons. In December 29th 1970, Constabulary Lieutenant Victor Corpus entered the Philippine Military Academy riding in a military vehicle. He was accompanied by two cars containing nine guerrillas that he earlier linked up with at Baguio City's Burnham Park. This group moved to the academy's armoury where they subdued the guards and stole 21 automatic rifles, fourteen carbines, six machine guns, several grenade launchers, a bazooka and over 5,000 rounds of ammunition into the waiting vehicles. The group drove to Cauayan town located in Isabela province where they linked up with NPA Commander Dante in the Sierra Madre Mountains. Corpus's defection was a national story, and caused Marcos to become wary of future plots by members of the AFP.

The NPA claimed to have killed over a dozen American military members and close to 200 government soldiers and policemen by 1970, the government did not dispute the number of AFP/PC deaths. NPA sought to create multiple fronts across the archipelago to tie down the government, and wear them out in a long struggle, as opposed to the failed Central Luzon strategy the Huks had used. In 1970, NPA cadres moved to the Eastern Visayas to create a rebel front. The Visayas offered rugged terrain which made the island good to conduct guerrilla warfare. By 1971 the NPA moved into Isabela, in North East Luzon, where the mountains and impoverished population were conducive to NPA operations. This helped the NPA establish a secure base.

Tactically the AFP began to emulate the US Army approach from Vietnam and, including the forced re–settlement of the population from areas with insurgent activity to government areas, and the use of free–fire zones. This meant that any individual located within a specified area was considered hostile. Military operations

Well armed MNLF rebels carrying a mix of weapons including Libyan supplied AK–47 and a captured M–16A1/M–203 combo, an M–14, and an M–1 Carbine. (via Albert Grandolini)

were relatively large in size and regularly caused plenty of "collateral damage' – which ran counter to the lessons many drew from the successful tactics against the Huks. Yet the AFP did not rely entirely on brute force, one of early experiments was to send small groups of soldiers into villages to create and oversee local militias. These militias were tasked with protecting villages from insurgents and local banditry and had the additional task of trying to reign in political militias tied to opposition parties. These units were initially made of five soldiers, who partnered with five civilians to form ten man teams. The Marcos regime also sought to disband militias linked to possible political opponents, as part of his strategy of centralization. These pro–government militias were controversial with newspapers warning of the risk that these units would provide a pool of manpower to set up a dictatorship. Allegations of human rights abuses and political meddling surfaced form the start of these projects.

Red Revolution

The insurgents sought to avoid direct contact with the AFP and the PC whenever possible. Having very few weapons – and then mainly those brought in by recruits from Tarlac Province – their early actions were limited to winning popular support, while offensive operations were undertaken solely with the purpose of capturing arms in small–scale ambushes and attacks on isolated military positions. For quite some

Marines loading a 57mm M–18 Recoilless Rifle. (via Albert Grandolini)

A PA M41 on training maneuvers. Seven were provided to the PA and proved incredibly useful in the fighting against MNLF insurgents. (via Albert Grandolini)

M114 155mm howitzer on display at Fort Magsaysay. (Author's Collection)

time, lack of armament was so severe, that the insurgent commanders had to impose a special set of rules to ensure that no arms would get lost or be recaptured by government forces.

In late September 1971 the NPA sent a delegation to the PRC to request weapons. Included on the list were hundreds of M–16 rifles, anti–tank rockets, mortars and anti–aircraft artillery. China instead offered over 1,000 Chinese made copies of the M–14 rifle, radios, mortars, anti–tank rockets and medical supplies – but no anti–aircraft weapons, in part because the NPA was too often on the run and unable make use of them.

A battalions sized force of AFP/PC was airlifted to Isabella in September in response to a platoon sized ambush by insurgents who killed six soldiers and damaged two helicopters. The additional troops quickly overran several NPA camps and took several prisoners. In November 1971 three PA battalions launched a major offensive against the NPA based in Isabela province. The offensive lasted until March 1972, destroying much of the NPA infrastructure. Additional

fighting broke out in late summer 1972 as over 7,000 PA/PC troops launched further assaults against insurgent infrastructure in the province. Despite AFP assaults, the NPA attempted to maintain their organization in the province.

The next problem was that of delivery: the communists requested deliveries with help of Chinese Navy's submarines, which Beijing deemed too risky. Instead, the Chinese provided money for the NPA to buy a fishing boat that would be used to ship arms to Luzon. Named, MV Karagatan, this boat arrived on 4 July 1972 with over 1,000 rifles, thousands of rounds of ammunition and few mortars, and put down her anchor around 300 metres offshore. The process of unloading proved extremely complex, and the boat was located by an U–17 several days later, sounding alarm in Manila. The PhAF was ordered to scramble and it deployed jet fighters, T–34s, UH–1s, and U–17s to attack and sink the boat and NPA insurgents near the beach, while the Army attempted to follow on the ground. Bad weather held up the AFP, allowing the NPA several days to try and unload as much as possible. The skipper of Karagatan ran his boat aground while attempting to evade air strikes, but when a PN tugboat arrived to tow her away, fire from insurgents on the beach injured the Navy's captain. When the weather cleared UH–1Hs brought in ground forces who clashed with the insurgents, losing four of their own number. The AFP troops were pushed back by the insurgents temporarily. The next day F–5s, UH–1s, and PN warships attacked the insurgents. Additional insurgents arrived but were forced back by the AFP. The surviving insurgents broke into small groups and fled. The Army was able to take most of the supplies, which included 900 small–arms, six M–40 recoilless rifles and 160,000 rounds of ammunition. The ship later sank in a storm.

Moro Revolt

While the AFP was busy fighting the NPA, the MNLF slowly grew in size to about 2,000 combatants. The armed wing of the MNLF was commanded by a field marshal who commanded provincial field marshals and zone commanders. MNLF control over Moro fighters was based on their access to foreign support and Libyan arms. The majority of the political leaders were based overseas and thus cut off from day to day contact with their commanders. The leadership of the armed wing was drawn from several sources – young men who had received training overseas or through government ROTC programs, criminals, outlaws and traditional tribal elite. Three groups of Moro fighters were sent to Sabah for training in guerrilla tactics from 1969 to 1974. The first group had 90 insurgents, the second group had 300 and the third group had 87.

By 1971, the MNLF began launching major attacks. Due to the large space the AFP was forced to fight across, aerial transportation became critical. Rapid troop deployments both to the theatre of operations and within it were facilitated by the acquisition of numerous transport aircraft such as Fokker F–27s and additional C–47s and Bell UH–1D/ UH–1H helicopters. Thirty–four UH–1s were received between 1968 and 1971, which facilitated the transport of the troops in combat. The UH–1H quickly showed its use in combat operations. It was also used in PhAF service at times as a gunship for CAS. Airmobile assaults were limited in size and frequency due to the small size of the fleet. Already in late August 1971 two helicopters were destroyed on the ground by an NPA sapper unit.

The 6th, 7th and 9th TFS rotated detachments through Matcan AFB to provide CAS and to conduct *reconnaissance* missions. Over the course of thousands of sorties several planes were struck by enemy fire, a few were shot down and others crashed for various reasons. The first F–5 to be hit occurred in 1972 when one was struck in the dorsal fin by MNLF fire. In 1972 there were six F–5As on operations based out of Matcan, until they were recalled from operations and replaced by F–86Fs. Some eleven additional T–33s were also acquired for the ongoing campaign while Taiwan donated eight additional F–86Fs.

In addition to the ground attack capabilities, the PhAF also needed to develop its *reconnaissance* and observation assets. For this purpose, two RT–33As, *reconnaissance* versions of the T–33 trainers, were supplied in 1970. The PhAF Air Depot also modified one C–47 for *reconnaissance* missions, equipped with an RC–8 camera installed inside the fuselage for vertical shooting. The Americans also delivered an EC–47Q that was used to fly radio–intercept missions and pinpoint the locations of the guerrilla wireless stations. The small number of Cessna O–1s and Stinson L–5s, serving as FAC, were considerably reinforced by the delivery of 28 Cessna U–17A/Bs in 1969. They equipped the 601st Liaison Squadron at Sangley Point. The FACs would fly with rockets either marking targets for other planes or conducting air strikes of their own. The Americans also handed over thirty de

A Marine M–60 team. (via Albert Grandolini):

Marine V–150 APC. (via Albert Grandolini)

Havilland DHC–2s, ex South Vietnamese planes, which arrived in July 1972 to support logistics. The first DHC–2s served with the 290th Special Missions Group. The versatile DHC–2s were used not only for logistics work and medical evacuation but were on occasion used for ground attack missions being fitted with bomb racks.

Several types of PhAF planes were hurriedly locally modified to provide much needed CAS. Three T–33s were fitted for 12.7mm machine guns and wing pylons for bombs and rockets, six U–17s were fitted with two 12.7mm machine guns, one T–34 was fitted for four 12.7mm machine guns and one HU–16 was armed with 12.7mm machine guns and rockets. Several different configurations were employed for the arming C–47s; nine AC–47s were fitted with three to four 12.7mm machine guns, three more were fitted with ten 12.7mm machine guns, one was fitted as a bomber. In total some sixty–five planes were modified to provide CAS. Internally the PhAF developed the ability to repair damaged airplanes and brought several seemingly derelict UH–1s, three T–34s and four C–47s back into service.

Farther south, in mid–1972, the Regional Air Command in Mindanao (RACMIN) had two AC–47 gunships, six UH–1Hs, DHC–2s, and U–17s. All of these planes were fitted out for CAS operations, with the C–47s providing the added benefit of being capable of night operations, through the use of flares.

Introduction of Martial Law

Despite large American assistance and enormous efforts of the armed forces, the rebellions by 1972 the worsened to such a degree allowing the government on September 21st 1972, after a false flag attack on General Enrile by alleged Communists, to justify declaring Martial

A fully–armed T–28Ds on the flight line. The first T–28Ds, of what would eventually be more than 55 to pass through the 15th SW, arrived in October 1974 entering service with the 16th Attack Squadron. The T–28 was the backbone of PhAF tactical aviation during the 1970s and 1980s, serving until July 1992. (via Albert Grandolini)

A rocket pod equipped SF–260WP in flight. The SF–260WPs arrived in kits in late February 1975 and entered service with the 17th Attack Squadron which had been formed in October 1974. (via Albert Grandolini)

Law. The declaration of martial law is still controversial as it became used to silence opposition to Macros and enabled him to rule, with the support of the AFP and PC, as a dictator for the next fourteen years. Martial Law allowed Marcos to take and hold power successfully but it also worked as a strong recruitment tool for anti government insurgents as any form of legitimate protest had been outlawed. Government propaganda had turned the NPA and MNLF into major threats, which they rapidly grew into being. Despite the declaration of martial law the number of insurgents in the field continued to grow. Thousands of college radicals flocked to the NPA, boosting it from a group numbering less than 1,000 members and around 300 small arms[6] to having within several years over 10,000 members and widespread popular support.

In Mindanao the declaration had the effect of making previously undecided Moros join the MNLF. The MNLF soon counted around 30,000 guerrillas,[7] who were supported by Libya and controlled the majority of the province of Cotabato and much of the Sulu archipelago. Around 70percent of the armed forces were tied down fighting the MNLF stretching the military to its limits. Around 100 soldiers a month were killed or wounded leading to desertions by soldiers. In time the situation became so bad that T–28As and T–34s from the flying school were forced into action conducting CAS operations in support of the Army and Marines. These propeller planes quickly proved themselves as useful in providing CAS to Army and Marine units and over the next few years it would be slower converted trainers which would bear the brunt of CAS support for ground operations.

Battle of Sibula Hill

The power of the PhAF was shown during the battle of Sibula Hill on the Island of Sulu in November 1972. MBLT2 was tasked with seizing the hill from the MNLF, which had fortified the position. On 26 November they made their first push against the hill, which was repulsed; giving the Marines their first defeat. Additional troops were brought in to take the hill, in the form of Scout Rangers. After taking the hill during a month of fighting a battalion of Marines were trapped by the MNLF and were under risk of being wiped out by the guerrillas. While the Marines dug in the PhAF was called on to prevent a massacre of the Marines. The PhAF moved over 60 fixed and rotary wing planes to the area and conducted day and night air strikes and

drops of supplies to the besieged Marines. The close range of the battle prompted the PhAF to fly in Colonel Pompeyo Vasquez to coordinate the air strikes from the ground. F–5s, F–86Fs, T–33s, T–34s, AC–47s and UH–1Hs, aided by on the FACs, were used in the operation to smash the MNLF forces and rescue the Marines. UH–1Hs were used to pull the Marines out that night.

During 1972 the MNLF conducted a series of offensives seizing control of multiple districts in Cotabato province. The AFP brought in additional troops and heavy weapons and with the use of superior firepower forced out the MNLF. The PhAF deployed AC–47s, U–17s and UH–1Hs, under the Composite Air Support Force Cotabato, to break the siege of Cotobato City and support a counter attack by government forces. The MNLF surrounded the city but government forces remained in control of the airport, which was ringed by enemy positions. Control of the airport was critical as thus the city was not fully cut off from government support. During the siege, the government claimed the MNLF lost 187 men while the government suffered 30 killed and 27 civilians killed.

The PhAF provided vital support for the Army and Marines as they took back town after town from the MNLF as the UH–1s moved troops around and attacked MNLF troops. From March to August the PhAF was tasked with supporting the government offensive on the MNLF strongholds as well as attacking sea borne MNLF reinforcements and supply ships. The town of Maganoy was retaken with a surprise airmobile assault using six UH–1s which landed troops from the 22nd IB. The UH–1s had to execute a tight spiral, one after the other, from 5,000 feet to a marked landing spot at the main square. On 6 April Maganoy was declared back under government control. Firepower in the form of airpower, artillery and armour was allowing the AFP to win positional engagements and the advantage of control of the skies allowed them to move troops around where needed.

Reorganization of the AFP

The scope and size of the conflict had caught the military off guard. The military which had prepared for a conventional conflict had been unready to conduct operations across the archipelago. All branches of the AFP were forced to expand in manpower and equipment to meet the needs of the threat. The PhAF, with its focus on conventional conflict, was especially hard hit. The jet fighters lacked the range and low speed agility to conduct the type of CAS needed; and were far more expensive to operate. Earlier in the conflict training planes had been pressed into action supporting ground operations, which became a model for CAS operations. The AFP also saw a need for additional transport planes.

The AFP grew from 45,000 in 1967 to 164,000 by 1977. The Army itself expanded from 13,500 in 1970 to 61,000 a decade later. This growth allowed the AFP to operate over much more of the countryside and keep some semblance of reserve and mobile forces to conduct

---

6 . According to General Enrile the NPA numbered between 400-900 full time members while Marcos officially claimed 1,028 members during the declaration of Martial Law.

7 . In 1973 the MNLF had close to 15,000 full time members in their armed wing, a figure which doubled by 1975.

PA soldiers on patrol. (via Albert Grandolini)

Members of the 1st Scout Ranger Company posing with an M–113 APC. As can be seen 1970s fashion penetrated AFP combat units, note the long hair and civilian articles of clothing such as blue jeans being sported by these Scout Rangers. (Via Lt. Colonel Dennis Eclarin)

major operations. Infantry divisions reorganized to handle COIN operations. *Reconnaissance* units were formed to conduct aggressive patrolling operations similar to the Scout Rangers. Infantry Divisions also formed civil affairs coordinating offices to work with local authorities in reinforcing government control and undertaking public works projects. Yet with the massive growth came discipline problems; human rights violations, wide spread corruption, drunkenness, and robbery became more common. This was a much different force than the small, non–political and well–led AFP from a decade earlier.

The HDFG(A) was expanded to five B–Teams and an HQ Company, it's units being deployed to work with pro–government militias. By 1978 it had grown to nine Companies. With the assistance of HDFG(A) trainers the Scout Rangers were reformed as a combat unit, numbering five companies in the Scout Ranger Group (SRG) by the end of the decade. Its units conducted long range patrols and direct action raids against insurgents. Often operating with military intelligence assets they aimed to strike at NPA leadership.

Light armoured unis in support of infantry proved of great use against the MNLF in positional clashes. Several half track personal carriers dating from the Second World War were deployed on operations. The PC made use of Second World War vintage M8 Greyhound armoured cars and M–3 half–track APCs to support their combat operations. Additional armored equipment was received including; forty–one FV–101 Scorpion light tanks in 1977 from England, sixty tracked M113 APCs between 1970 and 1979. The decade also saw the arrival of Portuguese V–200 four wheeled APCs,

capable of carrying a rifle squad. The field artillery was increased with a battery of eight M114 155mm howitzers in 1971, and seventy M30 107mm heavy mortars in 1973. AFP ground units also received new M–16A1s, M79 grenade launchers and M–60 machine guns to replace the Second World War vintage small arms, which went to militia and second line units.

The Philippine Navy itself went through a massive built up with the fall of South Vietnam, not just from the United States but with the arrival of ex–SVN Navy warships which in 1975 fled with crews and their families to the Philippines. The Philippines received seven Barnegat patrol frigates, one Cannon patrol frigate, seven PCE patrol corvettes, one Admirable class minesweeper, three LSI, four LSM and three LST–1s. From the USA and Japan came three Cannon class patrol frigates, ten LST–1s. Thus in the span of a year three Cannon frigates, seven Barnegat frigates, seven PCEs, one Admirable, thirteen LSTs and other ships entered service. These frigates and corvettes were far from cutting edge, dating back to the Second World War, but they represented a massive upgrade in capability for the PN and played a major role in the island fighting; providing fire support, patrols and troop movements. Six additional HU–16Bs were supplied in 1976 and 1977 as well for search and rescue and maritime patrol planes.

The conflict also resulted in expansion of the Marine Corps. At the start of the conflict it consisted of only three infantry companies with supporting units, it was reinforced by a fourth company in 1970. Three additional Marine companies were added the next year and two more in 1972. As local commanders began issuing specific calls for deployment of the Marines, the Corps was further expanded and reorganized into two battalions in 1973. This force was further expanded through the establishment of a third battalion, later that year, while the Scout Raider Platoon was used as a cadre for establishment of the 1st *Reconnaissance* Company. The German made UR–416 was tested by the Marines and was found very successful and was recommended for purchase, but was not acquired. In May 1975 LVTP–5 and LVTH–6s, surplus from the US, were received by the Marines and V–150s were received later in the year. In this fashion, the small 'ground force of the PN', rapidly became one the AFP's main shock forces, able of conducting amphibious operations and small unit patrolling deep within areas under insurgent control.

Marcos finished consolidating local police functions using the PC which numbered around 42,000 and the Integrated National Police (INP) which had around 65,000 members. The PC didn't fall under the INP for economic and military reasons; American aid to the police had been cut and thus the PC remained under the control of the AFP, despite their law enforcement role, to get access to American aid. The PC set up fearsome domestic intelligence agencies which specialized in torture and political repression such as the Fifth Constabulary Security Unit. These organizations stayed far from the battlefield but ruthlessly targeted suspected anti–Marcos activities among students, union activists and other civilians. The murder and display of victims by the PC was referred to as "salvaging" and had a serious effect on insurgent support networks and served to intimidate the opposition.

In 1976 to secure control of rural areas, the government ordered the establishment of a pro–government militia; the Integrated Civilian Home Defense Force (ICHDF). Command of the militia fell to the Army and PC. Existing militias connected with political rivals were disarmed or co–opted by the new organization. Initially training and pay were almost non–existent and it did not take long for the force to be marred by allegations of human rights abuses. Furthermore, they also became an excellent source of equipment for both the MNLF and the NPA who would raid outposts and capture weapons with often little resistance. Some ICHDF units under Special Forces command

An armed T–28D displaying four 70mm rocket pods and two 12.7mm machinegun pods. The T–28s were heavily armed for their size and their low speed enabled the crews to drop ordinance with excellent accuracy. The T–28 was another fixture of COIN operations in South East Asia, also seeing combat service in Thailand, Laos, Cambodia, and both North and South Vietnam. (via Albert Grandolini)

became excellent assets for the government, knowing the local terrain and the ere able to aggressively combat NPA infiltration freeing up combat units for frontline action. Within a decade over 100,000 militiamen were active in the countryside under the effective control of local political powerbrokers.

The PhAF began reorganizing itself as well. Different PhAF units were distributed into Composite Air Support Forces (CASF) which controlled CAS assets in a given region. The 1st and 2nd Air Divisions controlled the CASFs in the north while the 3rd Air Division controlled CASF in the south. Furthermore, the PhAF established a dedicated COIN unit, the 15th Strike Wing (15th SW), in November 1973, the mission of which was to provide CAS and conduct aerial interdiction in support of the large operations. The organizational structure and equipment of the unit was optimized for the CAS role. The airplanes initially assigned were six T–34As and six T–28As drawn from the 100th Training Wing and the 5th Fighter Wing. These aircraft were a sort of placeholders, because the PhAF was expecting to receive Vietnam War surplus T–28Ds and locally assembled SF–260WP trainers from Italy to provide teeth to the unit.

The first four combat ready and crewed T–28Ds were deployed in February 1975 to support operations near Zamboanga City. The SF–260s were deployed a few months later and were thrust into combat as well. The 15th SW was further improved in the next year through the arrival of a HU–16 flying boat which was to serve as a FAC and SAR platform and the transfer of a C–47 which was used to support the deployments. In 1976 the 25th Attack Squadron was formed using T–28s and served in the Western Command to not only provide air support for ground units and the PN and also to conduct *reconnaissance* patrols over the disputed Kalayaan Islands. The creation and deployment of the 15th SW took the burden off of the F–86s and F–5s.

The PhAF between 1972 and 1977 had become massively reinforced in transportation and liaison planes, which were vital as the war in the south worsened. Among the most important assets were the Bell UH–1H helicopters and old but dependable C–47 transports. The

An U–17 FAC seen while in the process of being armed with 70mm rockets. (via Albert Grandolini)

transport fleet was boosted through the arrival of C–130s, C–123s, N–22s and BN–2s. The 220th Heavy Airlift Wing based at Mactan Air Base in the centre of the Visayas, had three heavy transport squadrons (HTS). The 222nd HTS was activated in April 1973 on the new C–130 Hercules. The unit took on charge the first four L–100–20s with an additional C–130H which arrived later that same year. The next year two additional C–130Hs arrived, bringing the fleet to seven Hercules. The heavy transport wing other assets was the 221st and which operated seventeen C–123Ks received between 1973 and 1975 as well as the 223rd ATS with sixteen GAF N22Bs. The Nomads, deliveries of which began in October 1975, had self–sealing fuel tanks and wing hardpoints, and were the first overseas military sale of the Australian utility transport.

The other main transport unit was the 205th Composite (Airlift) Wing at Nichols Air Base, Pasay City, and including the 206th and 207th Air Transport Squadrons with respectively Fokker F–27s and C–47s. Most of the 29 BN–2 Islander light transports and utility planes from England also served with the wing, with some airframes being tasked for liaison duties with the 15th SW. The BN–2 was also used

Moro insurgents in civilian clothes with locally web gear to hold their magazines. Several of the insurgents carry Libyan supplied FN–FALs. (via Albert Grandolini)

in the maritime patrol mission by the PN. Six additional HU–16Bs were supplied in 1976 and 1977 as well maritime patrol and operated by the 27th Search and Rescue Squadron. Apart from the fixed–wing element, the 205th had numerically much larger helicopter component comprising in 1978 some forty–seven Bell UH–1Hs and three MBB BO–105s. They operated with the 210th Helicopter Squadron and the 505th Air Rescue Squadron.

In order to supervise the numerous detachments of light transports, FAC and light attack aircraft, it was decided to set up the 240th Combat Wing at Sangley Point. The unit had under its control the 291st Special Air Mission Squadron with 18 DHC–2s, the 901st Weather Squadron on Cessna 210s and 310s, and the 601st Liaison Squadron with 16 Cessna U–17A/Bs and O–1s. There was also the 303rd Air Rescue Squadron with eleven AC–47 gunships.

Long and Bloody Battle

The fighting during the Moro war was less focused on hearts and minds and more focused on the attempt to defeat a large and increasingly well equipped rebel army. Flush with Libyan arms, with a secure Sabahan base camp and with a large pool of willing volunteers the MNLF seized control of large areas quickly. There were reports that Libya had furnished SA–7 MANPADs to the insurgents, however, there was no confirmation for this, and no missiles were ever seen or captured.

During fighting in Panamao, Sulu during November 1972 the 4th company of MBLT2 holding a blocking position faced a major assault by the MNLF, resulting in 15 Marines KIA in exchange for 55 insurgents. During the fighting the Marines made use of a locally made armoured vehicle, Lakas–Loob[8] (Guts), to support ground operations.

8   An up armored 3/4-ton truck.

In November 1972 the vehicle was deployed supporting the 7th and 8th Marine Companies in their relief of the 4th Company. The two companies were pinned down by enemy fire and the vehicle provided essential services bringing as food and ammunition to front line units.

The MNLF conducted a series of offensives seizing control of several districts in Cotabato Province on the Island of Mindanao. The insurgents operated in a conventional manner holding fixed positions and trench lines giving the AFP much easier targets. The AFP deployed troops and heavy equipment and with the advantage of superior firepower and training forced the MNLF out several of the districts. The MNLF surrounded Cotabato City in 1973 but the AFP remained in control of the airport which was critical in keeping the city supplied. The PhAF deployed AC–47s, U–17s and UH–1Hs, under Composite Air Support Force Cotabato, to break the siege and support a counter attack by government forces.

The MNLF attempted to consolidate control over captured areas by building camps and holding towns. This led to sieges of rebel positions where the AFP was able to bring in artillery and air power to smash the insurgents. The insurgents surrendered their advantages in mobility to the AFP and allowed government troops to inflict heavy losses.

The PhAF was used during the war with the MNLF for all types of operations including *reconnaissance*, CAS, supply, air mobility, and strike. The PhAF attacked suspected rebel supply depots and hunted for supply ships used to aid the MNLF forces bring up supplies from the Sabah. The PhAF was vital in containing the MNLF uprisings, providing a degree of firepower and manoeuvre support the insurgents could not match. The PhAF was in many cases the only thing saving AFP units from the MNLF guerrillas. This led to a change in the PhAF to a more counter insurgency specific force with CAS and supply and mobility operations taking precedence over air defence. Conventional fighters were used in the ground attack role. In 1973 alone F–86Fs from the 9th TFS flew 123 strike missions over the war zone. In March 1973 the 7th TFS deployed a two plane detachment on Edwin Andrews AB in Zamboanga City.

By 1973 the combined PN–PhAF naval blockade had begun to show major results. The cut in supplies in turn forced some fronts to scale back actions as arms shipments were captured. Unfortunately for the AFP the PN and PhAF were simply not large enough to cover the waters. The PN despite its small size was not only used in patrolling and supply operations but saw operations on the gun line in support of ground forces. A Marine battalion on 8 July 1973 was pinned down on Basilan by MNLF fire which prompted the RPS Iloilo (PS–32) to move within 400 meters of the beach to bombard the coast in support of the Marines. A constabulary unit in a similar situation received fire support by the warship RPS Pangasinan (PS–31) and was then withdrawn on naval warships. Operations like this were common across the south as the navy conducted shelling and troop movements. The PN also operated small boats, which conducted coastal patrol and moved small units of ground troops.

The MNLF's first large offensive on Jolo overran the much of the island in late 1973. In holding back a major assault on Parang on 11 January 1974, an F–86F flown by Lieutenant Colonel Antonio Bautista, commander of the 9th TFS, suffered damage to his plane after making seven bombing and strafing runs over the exposed MNLF fighters and breaking up their advance. His landing gear failed to lower making a landing impossible. He attempted to jump over the airfield on Jolo. A change in the direction of the wing caused his parachute to land him in the middle of an MNLF force. UH–1Hs scrambled to rescue him were shot at by the insurgents and thus began a battle between the PhAF and MNLF. The UH–1Hs did return fire but there was no space large enough for them to land. Lieutenant Colonel Bautista lacked a survival radio or any other way to contact the UH–1Hs. A ground force moved forward to attempt to rescue him but when they arrived he had already been killed by MNLF forces.

PhAF airpower was decisive during the battle of Jolo City in January 1974. The town was held by elements of the PA's 1st Brigade, including its headquarters. Outside of the town a detachment of twenty Marines under orders to collect Moro firearms were ambushed. Several hundred MNLF insurgents then infiltrated the town over the preceding days and then a main force assault by close to 1,500 regulars overran the brigade's headquarters and took control of several key buildings. The brigade conducted a counter attack with over 5,000 soldiers and supported by artillery, gunboats and F–86Fs. There was additional support in the form of two M–41 light tanks stationed at the airport which provided stellar service. Hundreds of civilians were killed in the fighting along with some 200 insurgents, just under one hundred soldiers were killed. PhAF support was also vital during the battle for the town of Nuro. The town was held by a single HDFG(A) A–Team against several hundred Moro insurgents.

In other locations the MNLF insurgents relied on guerrilla tactics. In Cotabato the AFP forcibly resettled the population and relied on terror tactics to keep order. The insurgents began to harass government forces in and around Cotabato City. In June 1974 there was fierce fighting involving F–86 air strikes and artillery fired at MNLF insurgents who launched an attack against the Cotabato airport. Fighting near the airport involved mortar fire from both sides and small scale clashes.

The PMC made use of its new armour employing newly arrived LVTP–5 and LVTH–6s on 17 November 1975 at Tunling, Siasi, Sulu. Ground elements drawn from the 1st and 4th MBLTs backed by armored units consisting of twelve LVTs and three V–150s assaulted MNLF positions which fell under combined arms assaults. The insurgents showed little ability to fight armoured units.

Despite the control of the air and superior numbers, the AFP could not break the insurgents. In early March 1975 three AFP battalions on North West Basilan conducted a spoiling attack against a MNLF force estimated to number around 4000. By this point around 1750 AFP soldiers had already been killed in the fighting. Around 16,000 MNLF fighters were under arms but only half of them were available for operations at any time. During the fighting which followed, over 100 rebels were reported killed by the joint air, sea and land offensive. In December 1977 the PhAF finally located the MNLF headquarters in Zamboanga, and destroyed it in a devastating air raid. This seemed to have been influential in bringing the Moros back to the negotiation table along with government talks with Libya which cut off the flow of arms to the insurgents. Subsequently the MNLF decided provisionally to lay down its weapons, though not to disarm. At this point both parties allowed the Libyan regime to broker Tripoli Agreement in December 1976, which allowed for the establishment of a Muslim autonomous region made up Basilan, Sulu, Tawi–Tawi, Palawan, and the Muslim areas of Mindanao; many of these areas lacked a Muslim majority. A referendum was nevertheless held in April 1977 which led to widespread rejection of the deal which in turn led to a resumption fighting and government punitive operations in 1977 In 1979 a Regional Autonomous Government in was set up in the Central and Western Mindanao regions.

The Marcos Regime did not fulfil its promises of autonomy for the Moslems in the South, the armed struggle also restarted there in the early 1980s. The peace process, withdraw of arms supplies and political issues had split the Moro insurgents. A new force the Moro Islamic Liberation Front (MILF) was founded in March 1984 under Hashim Salamat. They took a more "Islamist" ideological position and

Two NPA insurgents wearing web gear fabricated in insurgent camps. The AK–47 is likely from the batch of arms delivered to Moro insurgents by Libya and not from external communist sources. (via Albert Grandolini)

ethnically were drawn from the Maguindanao Muslims who lived in Western and Central Mindandao.

Dissident Suppression Campaigns

In mid–1974, the AFP conducted an offensive against the NPA operating in Sorsogon. In Sorsogon the NPA operated in a heavy handed fashion against suspected government supporters in the area. The insurgents had attempted to turn the area into a self supportive base. Around 1,000 troops backed by the PhAF assaulted rebel held villages and blocked food from entering insurgent held area. The main NPA camp was surrounded, shelled and bombed from the air during the siege. By the end of the year the AFP had crushed the NPA in Sorsogon, of around 150 guerillas at the start of the action only ten remained in the field, the others had died, deserted or surrendered to the government. In March 1975 NPA forces in Aurora retreated from the province. One platoon sized group fought a running gun battle, some 50 clashes, for some 80 miles with PC Rangers, until reaching the Province of Nueva Ecija. Insurgents who remained in the province were effectively wiped out. The insurgents operating in the Eastern Visayas began to carry out platoon–size operations, which grew in frequency from 1975.

AFP assaults on the NPA kept them off balance on Luzon in 1975. In Isabela it was difficult for the insurgents to find food much less fight the AFP. Communications with the Central Committee were broken. The choice not to break out of Isabela came back to haunt the insurgents. Isabela had around 150 fortified pro–Government villages and dozens of AFP posts, which cut off the insurgents from the population. It was only in 1976 that the survivors attempted a break out. The breakout of Isabela went poorly as the insurgents were slowed by sickness, lack of food and the presence of children and pregnant women. Dozens died during the withdrawal – from sickness or from clashes with the AFP/PC. On reaching Cagayan they set up camp only to be attacked in 1978, with some 40 insurgents dying.

Major combined arms offensives by the army and PhAF destroyed several major NPA fronts. NPA positions were cordoned off, shelled and bombed and then filled with ground forces that would arrest and detain suspected insurgents. The Scout Rangers were deployed in small units to locate and destroy NPA bands, with considerable success.

By 1977 around 300 NPA insurgents in northern Luzon had been killed since 1970. The losses and the large PA/PC presence prevented Northern Luzon at that time from becoming a secure location for the rebellion. The NPA faced tensions between those commanders who

An AFP unit posing after conducting recoilless rifle and light mortar training. Through the 1980s the Korean War vintage 57mm remained in service and provided company level firepower with the 60mm mortar. (via Lt. Colonel Dennis Eclarin)

The M–18 was already outdated by the early 1950s as an anti–armor weapon but in the face of light armoured vehicles or light fortifications it remains reasonably formidable. (via Albert Grandolini)

SAF troopers, armed with Colt Model 653Ps and a Singapore made Ultimax–100, conducting anti–riot operations. The SAF thanks to its swing role in COIN and CT missions remains a favored unit with access to higher quality equipment than most units. Small numbers of Colt Model 653Ps were in service among elite units with the PA and SAF. (via Albert Grandolini)

wanted to first build an armed movement and those who wanted to focus on political organizing. CPP Chairman Jose Maria Sison pushed for a middle way focusing on creating grass roots support and an armed wing; by 1976 the NPA had around 1,000 firearms. Despite these successes by 1976 public support for Marcos was falling nationwide. The AFP/PC and pro–government militias were accused of brutality against the population, and widespread corruption hurt the economy.

President Marcos entered negotiations with the Communists, resulting in an armistice. This was broken, however, in the early 1976, when the NPA killed 36 soldiers in Jolo. The response of the AFP was fierce, the members of the HDFG(A) taking revenge on the local population and mining local roads, while the PhAF bombed suspected rebel bases in the area. With a precarious cease–fire agreed with the MNLF, the Philippines military divert more resources to fighting the NPA.

In August 1976, Bernabe Buscayno, aka Commander Dante, was arrested. The next year, CPP Chairman Jose Maria Sison was captured in La Union on November 10th 1977. These arrests crippled the high levels of the NPA. Yet exploiting peasant discontent the NPA was able to expand into other provinces. By this point the insurgents claimed to have possessed around 1,500 automatic weapons of various models.

On Samar, in December 1977, the AFP located the major rebel camp. For three days the PhAF bombed the camp and army artillery conducted around the clock shelling. The insurgents were forced to flee their camp. The insurgents changed their focus and attempted to set up a mobile structure, moving around to prevent being pinned down while mobilizing the population to support them. By 1979 the insurgents on Samar were among the most capable, both in terms of military potential and political support, front in the country. The insurgents and party officials who survived the government offensives

of the 1970s formed the core of a movement which over the next decade would rise to the level of becoming the major threat to the government.

CHAPTER 4
CORRUPTION, INCOMPETENCE AND POVERTY

In the years after 1975 American aid began to slow. Even though aid grew slightly under President Carter and Reagan, to a half a billion dollars a year, still the situation with the AFP began to get worse.

Dashed Hopes
The PhAF was at a crossroad with much equipment in needs to be replaced. Manila tried to maintain its air power capacities by trying to acquire new aircraft by direct purchases or by assembling them under license. Procurement fell under four main headings: free transfers

under the US Military Assistance Program (MAP), and credit purchases under favourable terms of the US Foreign Military Sales (FMS); cash purchases, nowadays primarily of non–US equipment; and local purchases under the Self–Reliance Development Program (SRDP). The key to the SRDP acquisition process was the fledgling local aircraft industry, the National Aero Manufacturing Corporation (NAMC). The NAMC started its activities by assembling the German MBB BO–105 helicopter and the British BN–2 Islander. With those new industrial capabilities, ambitious plans had been drawing out not

A training patrol with the characteristic long hair which remained popular in AFP service during the 1970s and 1980s. (via Lt. Colonel Dennis Eclarin)

A truck mounting an M60 machine gun and M18 recoilless rifle with a V–150 in the background. (via Albert Grandolini)

only to furnish aircraft to the PhAF but also for the Navy and the Army.

By the end of the 1970s, the Navy had set up a small air component with five BO–105s and five BN–2. Seven of the PN small fleet of frigates were, in fact, transferred from the South Vietnamese Navy after the collapse of the Saigon regime in 1975. Four of the frigates were fitted with helicopter decks while the service was also trying to acquire six maritime patrol aircraft needed for surveillance–submarine detection in the crucial area west of Palawan and in the Mindanao approaches. The PhAF did not want to relinquish the maritime patrol role and it acquired three Fokker F–27MPAs in 1982 that were used by the 221st Airlift Squadron of the 220th Airlift Wing.

By early 1979, the PhAF was struggling to fulfil its missions, including the air defence task. It was felt that the F–5A and the obsolete F–86F could no longer be considered as credible platforms for intercepting transport aircraft smuggling in supplies for the insurgents at night. Since the early 1970s, the PhAF Intelligence suspected that Chinese aircraft had flown supply missions, even though the American forces in the Philippines denied this. In 1978, second hand F–8H Crusader was selected under the FMS. The $11.7 million contract placed in late 1977 covered 35 planes. And under a separate contract, 25 of these were completely refurbished prior delivery, the remaining ten being cannibalized as part of a ten year–spares program. A nucleus of PhAF instructors was trained by Vought on a TF–8A two–seat trainer which was leased from NASA. The refurbished airframes reequipped the 7th FS at Basa from August 1978 on. From the start there were issues with the F–8s; they were expensive to fly, maintain and were of little use against the guerrillas The F–8 was only plane in the PAF which could drop 2000lb Mk.84 bombs and make use of the Bullpup guided missile, though they served strictly in the air defense role. In the early 1980s the F–8s were fitted with AIM–9Bs supplied for the F–5s. By the mid–1980s the F–8Hs were getting costly to keep in the air due to age and rising fuel costs and were increasingly grounded. The transport fleet rapidly shrank from its peak in the 1970s. The remaining C–47s were phased out from PhAF service in the 1980s as it was thought to be too expensive to refit them with new engines, as a consequence the AC–47s were also taken out of service from 1976 on. The C–123K transport planes were phased out of service in 1982 because it became too difficult to acquire spare parts for them while the three remaining C–130H themselves suffered from serviceability issues.

The helicopter fleet was not in much better shape. The fleet remained small, and airmobile movement became increasingly rare. Eighteen UH–1Hs were received in 1980 with an additional 15

UH–1Hs received in 1982. The additional UH–1Hs brought the totals received, minus the heavy attrition, to 75 UH–1H models and six UH–1Ds of which some 28 were operational. Two Bell 212s and two Bell 214s were also placed in service in 1977 and 1982 respectively, alongside two Hughes 300s. In 1979, two SA–330 Puma helicopters were supplied to the PhAF, for VIP missions, followed in 1983 by two Sikorsky S–70A–5 Blackhawks.

The PA pushed for the creation of a wing–sized battlefield helicopter unit which would remove need to rely on PhAF helicopter support. The projected Army Aviation Battalion was to consist of three helicopter companies; each equipped with 20 UH–1Hs; one company of a modern gunship helicopter (BO–105 or AH–1 Cobra) for fire support; and a maintenance unit. The PhAF strongly resisted this plan which would cut into its funding. Inter–services rivalry meant that the PN air branch remained small while a combat capable Army Aviation Corps was never created.[9]

Some F–5As and T–28Ds received new radios, allowing direct communications with ground troops. The 15th SW which was still at the forefront of operations, was forced to disband the 25th Attack Squadron in 1983 for a shortage of personnel and equipment and the 17th Attack Squadron in 1985 was disbanded for financial reasons leaving the 16th Attack Squadron as the only assigned unit. The S–76s were used as VIP helicopters and for search and rescue while the AUH–76s were used as gunships in the 15th SW alongside the T–28s. A new unit, the 20th Air Commando Squadron (ACS), was formed in 1984 to operate the fourteen Sikorsky AUH–76 gunships while the 15th SW took control of the 205th Helicopter Wing's 505th Air Rescue Squadron (ARS) which was equipped with three Sikorsky S–76s. Soon after entering service the AUH–76s saw action both in the South and in Luzon facing Moro and Communist insurgents.

Floundering Against the NPA

The communist insurgents had grown in numbers and influence. Estimates of their numbers ranged from 12,500 to 20,000 and in the combat zone the government only had a four to one ratio which prevented them from massing numbers against the insurgents. The NPA was still small and relied on raids and ambushes but was increasingly able to conduct larger scale operations such as raids against military posts, police stations and towns. The NPA had around 8,000 full time guerrillas fighting in 43 of the nation's 73 provinces.

---

9   The PA at present has an aviation battalion equipped with around a half dozen single-engine Cessnas, three two-engine Beechcraft liaison plans and will be receiving two Short C-23 Sherpas. These plans conduct limited liaison work.

A heavily armed PA patrol. (via Albert Grandolini)

In 1981 the NPA began to lay the foundation of a regular army, organizing the different fronts and attempting to set up an army. In 1981 the NPA fronts on the Visayan Islands were ordered to transfer men to other fronts on different islands.

During the middle of the decade the NPA had begun a project of creating standing companies to combat the AFP on a larger scale. These companies often numbered only 70 to 80 men. These companies would be combined temporarily to form battalions for major operations. Each NPA company had between three and four platoons. Each platoon had a party branch to exercise control. There were shortages of trained officers, qualified in logistic and more bureaucratic tasks. Most officers were promoted from the ranks, moving up the chain of command which led to good knowledge of small unit operations but limited proficiency in more traditional staff tasks. NPA commanders also led generally from the front lines, causing a steady stream of losses among the best commanders. Camp locations in some regions were moved monthly to prevent AFP intelligence from locating them.

NPA conducting raids against isolated PA and PC posts. Typically the NPA would mass a large force, often outnumbering the defenders by some three or four to one, often disarming the garrison without a shot being fired. Ambushes were often conducting by first observing AFP patrols and their patterns over time and then positioning themselves on their typical advance routes. The raids and ambushes were conducted to capture weapons and to make a political point. The increase in attacks led to land owners in some areas to move, giving over land to their tenets, other land owners to stay in business raised wages to tenets. This gave the NPA political victories in the hearts and minds struggle.

PA V–150 APC on the streets of Manila. (via Albert Grandolini)

Arms supplies had been built up through raids on AFP units and private firearm owners. In some areas "revolutionary taxes" paid by peasants and landowners were to be paid, in bullets supplied to the NPA. The NPA lacked enough weapons to arm all of its followers, having some twelve thousand men under arms, but had enough followers in theory to triple its manpower had it possessed the weapons. The shortage of weapons, and more importantly ammunition, prevented larger scale operations, but the supply did allow for the increase in the size of attacks from squads to companies. Another major shortage was in the area of trained medical staff and supplies, shortages of qualified medical staff led to many guerrillas dying from treatable wounds.

Scout Rangers on parade carrying Colt 653s, some m ounting M–203 grenade launchers. By 1986 the SRR had around 2,500 men in four battalions, of three companies each, and an additional ten independent companies. (via Lt. Colonel Dennis Eclarin)

The NPA began to move to tactics involving urban hit squads, the so called Sparrow Units. These small three person teams would murder soldiers, pro–government militiamen of the CHDF, government officials and police officers. They also were a source of weapons, as the weapons of dead soldiers and police officers would be supplied to regular units of the NPA. NPA attempts to build ammunition in camps failed. Capturing ammunition in raids and ambushes could simply not keep a steady stream of ammunition to the insurgents. Thus the insurgents set to buying bullets from government forces. Capturing weapons was also a slow process; a successful raid might only set a single rifle or at best a couple, often of different types shooting different calibres.

AFP planning settled increasing on a hold, clear and build approach. This linked with a focus on small unit actions looked to hold promise and was part of a theoretical attempt to move away from conventional warfare tactics back to the same past successful tactics. More effective were intelligence operations aimed at infiltrating the insurgents with government agents. In time these actions would lead to bloody purges of rebel ranks.

A major issue hampering the AFP was a lack of tactical mobility. This prevented units from following up on successes rapidly and slowed down the reaction time to reinforce units under attack. Thus the guerrillas were often able to escape even when hit hard by the AFP. Often time's units would have to empress civilian transportation to provide mobility; most of the best equipment was tasked with protecting the Marcos regime. The other factor preventing the AFP from responding to raids on isolated posts was the fear of NPA ambush, NPA raiding parties would leave ambush teams to cover the roads. Thus isolated units often had the knowledge that if attacked

there would be no reinforcements arriving. Some garrisons worked out deals with the NPA to create local cease fires and other units took their frustrations out on the local population. Morale among many units was low. This poor state had an effect on younger officers, who began to blame the short comings on the Marcos regime.

Scout Ranger small unit actions became a model for other units in the AFP and was copied in the Constabulary in the form of the Special Action Force (SAF) which was a reaction force tasked with supporting counter insurgency and counter terrorism operations. The personnel were drawn from various units including the disbanded Constabulary Brigade, the Long Range Patrol Battalion, the K–9 Support Company, Special Organized Group, the Light Reaction Unit, and other Constabulary units. Yet the bulk of the other 180 Constabulary battalions were tied down in static defense across the country in small company and platoon sized positions which made tempting targets for rebel raids.

The SAF was tasked with conducting operations across the country. The unit was trained in airborne operations, with the majority of members being airborne and commando qualified, despite the lack of airborne operations. Special Action Companies "SAC" were sent to different islands to act as the reaction force for counter insurgency operations. Politically the creation of the SAF was an attempt by General Ramos to regain some influence as General Ver had disbanded the 11 Battalion Constabulary Brigade, which had been under the command of Ramos, and scattered the manpower to various provinces. The SAF provided Ramos with an elite battalion sized force for counter guerilla warfare and also to support him in the palace intrigues which defined the Marcos regime. In this endeavor,

Ramos was aided by Colonel Honasan, General Enrile's protégé, who supplied weapons and space to train for the new unit.

In 1986, the Scout Rangers were designated as a national maneuver unit, with four battalions and ten independent companies.[10] As such the unit was tasked with nationwide operations and got priority for transportation. Two battalions were located at the time in Bicol, one in Luzon and the other in Mindanao with three companies in Luzon, two in the Visayas, one in Luzon and the others being rotated through after retraining and refitting. The Scout Rangers were the teeth of the army's actions against the insurgents.

Marcos's distrust of the military led to the promotion of officers for their loyalty to the regime, caused anger by other officers, who often served in combat units. The enlargement of the PA, PMCs and CHDF was seen in the PC as a way of reducing their own influence over the last decade. Marcos had further formed a 15,000 man Presidential Security Command (PSG) with the role of protecting him from domestic opposition; troops who had no mission other than to protect the Marcos family.

In the summer of 1982 the AFP undertook a new large offensive against the communists, beginning the offensive through an airmobile operation conducted by the Special Forces against approximately one hundred insurgents with Agusan del Norte. In February 1983 a similar operation was undertaken against 600 communists in the north by Mindanao. In February 1983, two Scout Ranger Battalions (SRBs) were deployed to Mindanao, along with three infantry battalions to support Marine forces conducting operations against the NPA. These punitive expeditions were overshadowed by the assassination of the Philippine opposition leader, Benigno Aquino, on 21 August 1983, at Manila's international airport, an event which would haunt the Marcos regime until its end.

The military in 1984 began the concept of the Special Operations Team (SOT). These were units tasked with Special Forces style mission of winning the hearts and minds of villagers in the war zones. These twenty–man teams would live among villagers and provide services along with protecting them from rebel bands, and operated in a similar style to the NPA's seven–man propaganda team. Past sweeps left villages at the mercy of the NPA once army troops withdrew so the new strategy was to hold what villages were taken. The SOT's were initially formed under the 4th Division and their usage spread to other divisions used in concert with the militias. What made them different from the Special Forces Regiment was that the SOTs were a part of Infantry Divisions. Protection for the teams was provided by other infantrymen.

In late 1984 a series of major setbacks led to the NPA in Mindanao searching for spies within its own ranks. Several raids were intercepted by army units and other operations were simply botched. In the middle of 1985 the search for traitors started and by the end of the year the purge had gone out of control, spurred on by government intelligence operations. NPA members were executed for having failed past operations or were simply accused of being spies. The government claimed over 800 members had been killed in the purges; the NPA claimed only 60 members had been executed. Hundreds of guerrillas defected to the AFP and morale among the remaining Mindanao based NPA plummeted as mistrust spread throughout the ranks. Whatever the number this had a negative effect on the movement as

A standard seven–man Scout Ranger patrol, with several men equipped with the venerable M–14 7.62mm battle rifle. (via Lt. Colonel Dennis Eclarin)

Marines loading a 57mm M–18 Recoilless Rifle. (via Albert Grandolini)

PA soldiers in Manila. The soldier in the foreground carries an M–14 rifle, which remains popular in AFP service. (via Albert Grandolini)

the segments population saw the movement caught up in paranoia, similar to the Khmer Rouge. These purges and the assignation units made the NPA look more violent and less like the Robin Hood style outlaw they painted themselves as.

The PhAF supplied additional officers to ground units to provide liaison and to better coordinate the PhAF's role in operations – from coordinating air strikes to aiding in setting up combat detachments for different war–zones depending on the needs of ground forces. Over the summer of 1984 a major operation was launched by the 41st and 48th IB supported by a joint task force of Scout Rangers, Marines and the PC for a force of around three thousand men. With air support provided by T–28s and helicopters the AFP took control of villages in the Tinglayan and Betwagan municipalities through late June and early July. The operation was not without problems as

---

10 . Scout Ranger battalions numbered around five hundred men, each battalion had three companies of between eighty and one hundred men. The typical Scout Ranger patrol was seven men with two seven man patrols making a squad. Each seven-man patrol typically had one point-man, one radio man, one machine gunner, one medic, a patrol leader, a demolitions expert and a navigation specialist.

Despite the lack of external support NPA regular units are well equipped with personal weapons. (via Albert Grandolini)

Female NPA cadres. Homemade weapons like these shotguns are common among local guerillas freeing up more capable equipment for main force units. (via Albert Grandolini)

the government offensive prevented farming activities by the Ibaloi peoples. In late 1984 the Marines deployed over one thousand troops to Davao, which was in danger of falling to the NPA. The Marines functioned in a hearts and minds role in rural areas and worked with politically connected urban gangs which murdered suspected leftist dissidents. This rural hearts and minds approach mixed with an iron fist in the urban areas forced the NPA back in Davao.

In March 1985 the NPA scored a major coup, raiding a Coast Guard training centre in the Visayas and making off with 421 rifles. In May 1985 a detachment of Scout Rangers in Negros Occidental was raided by the NPA. The raiders attacked their headquarters in the town of Isabela, killing 12 Scout Rangers and wounding seven, for three insurgents wounded. The Scout Rangers had failed to post guards and lookouts and were caught off guard, and the NPA made off with 72 rifles and a machine gun. Large scale hauls like this were rare and generally weapons were acquired in small numbers.

While the NPA had survived for over 15 years, it was clear that the 12,000 insurgents were not winning. People's warfare dogma and considerable rural support was not enough to overwhelm the 350,000 man AFP/PC. They were still in the first stage of the Maoist warfare doctrine, and without external support seemed unable to defeat the Marcos Regime.

People to Power

Inside the army there grew military fraternities who opposed the rule of the country, yet where not against the idea of military rule. The Reform Army Movement (RAM) numbered by 1985 close to 300 officers drawn from the Philippine Military Academy (PMA). Officers from the Scout Rangers and Constabulary had begun planning a coup to remove the Marcos regime. Their complaints were not limited to allegations of corruption and human rights violations but included slow promotions, nepotism in promotion and lack of resources being diverted to the military. The revolt came to be led by two Generals; Juan Enrile and Fidel Ramos, both members of Marcos's inner circle. Enrile had turned against Marcos after being seen as a potential political rival and had his powers as Minister of Defense weakened, preventing him from even ordering the movement of troops.

The rebellion was nearly foiled by a double agent inside the RAM who reported to General Ver about the planned coup. Ver deployed Marines and other loyalist troops into positions to be ready to deal with the plotters. After RAM officers learned of government preparations the plotters took shelter in Camp Crame and Camp Aguinaldo. Ramos inside Camp Crame had 450 troops under his direct command and had the loyalty of PC troops across Metro Manila. The officers

changed their plans from a military coup to a mutiny by taking control of the airwaves. Support from anti–Marcos dissidents swelled the numbers as regular citizens, movie actors, and Catholic clergy came out to support the rebel soldiers.

Two UH–1 helicopters were located with the rebels but no attempt was made to destroy them on the ground through either air strikes or shelling because the risk of a battle breaking out and the inevitable losses to the civilian population caught between loyalist and rebel units would have led to widespread condemnation. The protestors were faced by battle hardened Marines under General Taidar. The mass of protestors was able to prevent the Marines from pushing into the camp. The commanders decided against shooting into or over the crowd to prevent massive civilian losses and found their way blocked at every path. AUH–76 gunships attempted to locate clear routes for loyalist troops.

On 12 March, the third day of the protests, a battalion of Marines supported by two AUH–76s were ordered to punch through the human walls near Camp Crane. The commander of the 15th SW Col. Antonio Sotelo was then ordered to assemble a mission to knock out to rebel helicopters at Camp Crane. The pilots of the AT–28s and AUH–76s were supportive of the military rebels, many of whom they had served with in past operations. Sotelo had requested rifles to arm ground crews to protect their airbase but in reality the rifles were to be issued to the pilots for their defection to the rebels. The order from General Ver for elements of the 15th SW to strike the camp was scrapped and Ver ordered them to fly *reconnaissance* missions over the area.

Colonel Soleto, the commander of the 15th SW, was not a supporter of the RAM but disliked General Ver and the path he thought the military was going down, this and a friendship with Ramos caused him to defect. The 15th SW initially followed orders to conduct patrols over the revolt to show loyalty to the government and to verify the allegiance of the crews, but were preparing to defect at the soonest possible time. Two helicopters were ordered to conduct patrols on the third day; the orders were not followed as seven AUH–76s of the 20th ACS led by Major Charles Hotchkiss joined by Colonel Soleto, the wing commander, joined the protestors and the rebel factions of the army at Camp Crame. The helicopters initially flew over the camp which alarmed those on the ground, worried about air strikes but on the second pass the helicopters landed and the confusion was cleared up. With the loss of the entire 15th SW and their commander Colonel Antonio Sotelo the Marcos regime lost the teeth of the PhAF.

North American F–51D Mustang armed with 5–inch rockets. The F–51D was the first tactical fighter employed by the PhAF in the post–war period and served extensively against Huk insurgents. Except for six machine guns calibre 12.7mm, usual armament consisted of six HVAR unguided rockets calibre 127mm, and bombs calibre 100 and 200lbs. Inset is showing the crest of the 5th Tactical Fighter Group – usually applied on the fin of Philippino Mustangs. (Artwork by Tom Cooper)

This UH–34D served with the 505 Air Rescue Squadron. Three were supplied to the PhAF still wearing their standard light grey colours overall, and large markings denoting their role as search and rescue helicopters. Nevertheless, they were modified to carry light bombs underneath forward fuselage too. (Artwork by Ugo Crisponi)

The PhAF made heavy use of its squadron of eleven AC–47s armed with machine–guns calibre 12.7mm during the height of the Moro revolt. Budgetary shortfalls and age of these venerable aircraft resulted in their withdrawal from service in the 1980s, along with cargo and ELINT variants. (Artwork by Tom Cooper)

North American T–28D (the type was nick–named Tora–Tora in PhAF service) from the early 1990s, by when some were waring this worn–out dark–green camouflage. The venerable T–28 trainer became the primary tactical strike plane from the mid 1970s through the early 1990s. Insets are showing the 12.7mm machinegun pod, BLU–27 napalm tank, LAU–7H pod for unguided rockets calibre 2.75in, and Mk.81 bomb. The T–28s also locally designed cluster bomb units which consisted of mortar grenades calibre 81mm. Inset is showing the crest of the 15th Strike Wing – usually applied on the fin of Philippino T–28s. (Artwork by Tom Cooper)

An F–86F Sabre (this example was nick–named 'Labuya') in the rarely photographed camouflage pattern adopted by units in the 1970s. The type was operated by the 5th Fighter Wing and initially tasked with air defense, for which AIM–9B Sidewinder missiles were installed. The Moro and Communists insurrections led to them being primarily employed in the ground attack role, armed with general–purpose bombs and unguided rockets. Several F–86s were lost on combat operations against the MNLF, though rumors regarding SA–7 usage appear to be unfounded. They were ultimately replaced by F–8 Crusaders, which did not see combat service.(Artwork by Tom Cooper)

One of 19 F–5As (and 3 F–5Bs) that entered service with the 6th Fighter Squadron of the 5th Fighter Wing, beginning in 1966, shown as most of the fleet appeared through the 1970s, when they were camouflaged in colours used for the USAF's standardized 'South–East Asia' camouflage pattern. The PhAF F–5s could be armed with typical weapons for this type, ranging from AIM–9B Sidewinders and Mk.82 bombs, to LAU–7H pods for unguided rockets. They saw their last action in the Year 2000, while conducting air strikes against Camp Abubakar with Mk.82 and M117 bombs. After their withdrawal from service, all radios, gun–sights, and cannons have been stripped off of derelict F–5s and installed on other aircraft. Insets are showing crests of the 5th Fighter Wing and the 6th Fighter Squadron. (Artwork by Tom Cooper)

An SF−260TP of the 15th Strike Wing carrying a seven round 70mm rocket pod. The first armed SF.260s entered service in the 1970s, initially in form of piston engined SF−260WPs. Through the 1990s, the fleet was so much worn out, that there was shortage of operational airframes. This forced the PhAF to press SF.260TPs from the 100th Training Wing into combat operations. Most of these aircraft were painted in this disruptive camouflage pattern, consisting of sand, dark green, dark brown, and black, and several wore prominent 'sharkmouth' insignia on engine cowling. Crest on the fin is that of the Philippine Air Force.(Artwork by Tom Cooper)

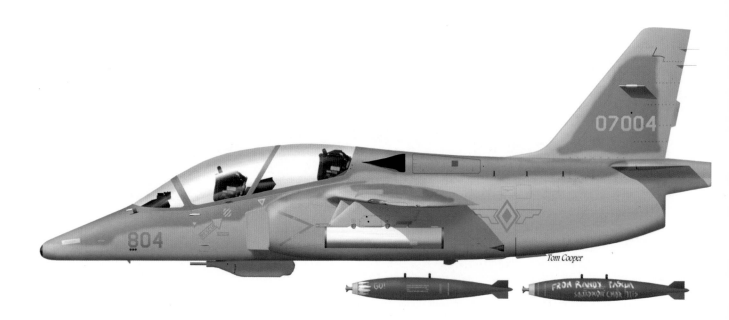

An S−211 of the 5th Fighter Wing fitted with a Aerotech Industries Philippines, Inc. designed 12.7mm machinegun pod under the centerline and a seven round 70mm rocket pod under each wing. With the retirement of the F−5s the handful of operational S−211s served as the only jet "fighters" in the PhAF until the Year 2015. They were equipped with radios and gun−sights taken from F−5s, and dubbed 'AS−211s'. Despite their air superiority camouflage the S−211s have been heavily deployed to provide CAS in operations against the BIFF. Insets are showing two Mk.82 bombs with typical inscriptions applied by ground crews of the 7th Tactical Fighter Squadron. (Artwork by Tom Cooper)

A PhAF UH–1H, no less but 200 of which were handed to the Philippines over the time, and about 80 of which remain in service currently. They are primarily deployed to transport commandos of elite ground units into raids against militants active in otherwise inaccessible areas.

Majority of UH–1Hs delivered to the Philippine Air Force were left in their olive drab colour, applied in the USA. At the height of the Moro Rebellion in the 1970s the UH–1s were sometimes deployed as helicopter gunships. Even today, when better equipped types are available, UH–1Hs are still frequently providing close air support with help of door–mounted machine guns. (Artwork by Ugo Crisponi)

The Philippine Air Force obtained 17 Sikorsky AUH–76 helicopters, 14 of which were deployed as helicopter gunships. This example was illustrated armed with a pod for 12.7mm machine gun installed on the cabin–side. Other typical armament includes seven–round LAU–7H rocket pods or pods with 7.62mm machine guns. (Artwork by Ugo Crisponi).

MD–520 light attack helicopters are operated by the 15th Strike Wing. They are usually armed with seven–round LAU–7H rocket pods and 12.7mm machine guns – one of which is often carried on each side of the helicopter (as shown here). PhAF MD–520s maintain a near permanent presence during AFP–operations, despite the small size of the fleet. In combat, they are usually teamed with OV–10As to provide close air support, or fly escort for UH–1Hs. (Artwork by Ugo Crisponi)

This M113 Fire Support Vehicle is shown as sighted during operations against the MILF in the Year 2000. The installation of the turret from derelict Scorpion light tanks is a result of shortfall of close fire support vehicles. In early 2014, the PA announced intention to modify 14 additional M113s in similar fashion. Notable is almost complete absence of any markings – except the 'licence plate', applied in white on the left front side of the fender. (Artwork by Tom Cooper)

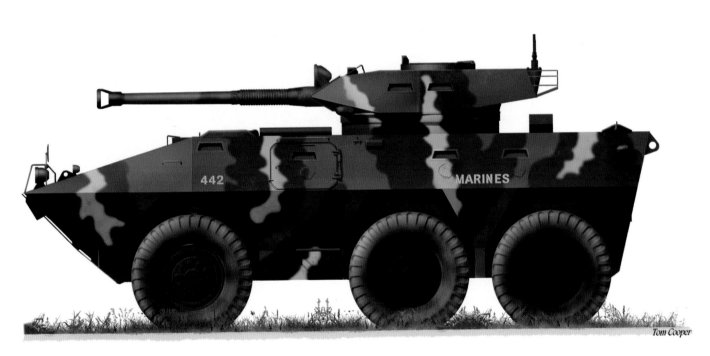

One of Cadillac V–300 armored cars armed with the 90mm cannon, as operated by the Philippine Marines. While highly vulnerable to insurgent RPG–2s the V–300 provides a unique fire support capability for the Marines, as the 90mm main gun is the largest direct fire system that is deployed on COIN operations. (Artwork by Tom Cooper)

Philippine Marines are also operating Cadillac V–150 armored cars. Usually in service with the Marine Ready Force, they are stationed close to Manila with counter–coup operations as their primary mission. This vehicle was modified through installation of a turret for 7.62mm machine gun over the rear part of the troop compartment. (Artwork by Tom Cooper)

The Philippine National Police's Special Action Force is also operating a number of V–150s, some of which are meanwhile sporting digital camouflage, and 'personal' names, as illustrated here. Between others, these vehicles were deployed to support Philippine Army's SAF troops during operations to disarm Ampatuan Clan CVOs, in 2009, and against MNLF insurgents in 2013. Primarily serving as traditional APCs, they are sometimes deployed as surrogate tanks, to provide fire support for ground troops. (Artwork by Tom Cooper)

Rebel troops being detained on a PN LST. (via Albert Grandolini)

A patrol of Scout Rangers on operations in Kalinga Apayao. (via Lt. Colonel Dennis Eclarin)

A lightly equipped patrol from the 5th SRC wearing OD style camouflage posing next to a PhAF UH–1H helicopter. Despite the coup attempts and political instability combat operations continued. (via Lt. Colonel Dennis Eclarin)

The rebel soldiers now had an air force made up of seven AUH–76s, two S–76s and one BO–105 along with the two UH–1Hs. Another BO–105 had attempted to defect but was stopped on the ground. The 15th SW T–28s had in meantime flown to the American Clark AFB, where they were unable to refuel and thus took not further part in the revolt. After these massive defections, two F–5As appeared overhead, with orders to bomb the camp. But after circling several times they returned to base: the pilots also supported the protestors.

The insurgents soon turned their AUH–76s against the government. One AUH–76, flown by Captain Wilfredo Evangelista, was sending to destroy the radio transmitter of the Malacanang Palace; unable to find the transmitter, the pilot was directed to damage the palace itself. He complied by firing six 70mm rockets into the room of the President's wife, Imelda Marcos. He then strafed and destroyed the Audi car fleet of Marcos's son in law.

Marcos had five UH–1Hs in the area which were given orders to ferry loyalist forces against the mutineers. The helicopters were to land two dozen Scout Rangers, armed with anti tank weapons and recoilless rifles, to attack the rebel airplanes. One of the helicopters was to fly General Cirilo Oropesa, who was to take control of a Marine artillery unit to shell the insurgents. The insurgents, discovering this, ordered the AUH–76s onto the offensive. They were to attack the UH–1Hs where ever they could be found; whether on the ground or airborne. Three AUH–76s departed to Bonfacio and found five UH–1Hs on the flight line being readied for takeoff. The AUH–76 crews called the ground crews and requested they withdraw before the air strike. After a few strafing runs the UH–1s were crippled while the C–130s, N–22s and F–27s at the airbase deliberately were left intact.

In the aftermath of this operation Marcos could no longer rely on airpower to strike the insurgents. The remainder of the 5th FW at Basa AFB in Pampanga also switched side, bringing ten operational F–5As, seven F–8Hs and five T–33s. Two F–5As conducted sorties over loyalist positions, yet were unable to fire their guns, pro–insurgents ground crews had disabled their firing mechanisms just in case any of the pilots remained loyal to Marcos. At night, Soleto moved his helicopters from Camp Crame to Clark AFB, worried about sabotage. He attempted to get fuel from Clark AFB, and after an impasse, the Americans allowed fuel to be supplied for the AUH–76s.

Marcos still had four personal helicopters, which he was unable to risk losing because that would cut off any escape route. The situations solved itself on its own, because their crews defected to the insurgents, loaving nobody behind to fly the helicopters. On the morning of February 25th, the fourth day of protests, three C–130s and two F–27s bringing in reinforcements to Manila landed instead at Clark and also

joined the rebellion. With the government falling apart quickly and American pressure calling for Marcos to allow a peaceful transition of power it became clear the Marcos regime was over. Four American HH–3Es were used to remove Marcos and his family to their eventual exile in Hawaii.

Problems with internal stability and resentment within the military remained in the subsequent years, despite the democratic development of the country. The United States continued to distance themselves more and more with the Philippines. Straightforward military aid gave way to a credit system that tied the country's resources to difficult repayment schemes. The PhAF consequently continued to shrink. Its new commander, Brigadier General Ramon Farolan, had the difficult task to reinstate the morale of his men and restore unity among the officers. Years of dictatorship and politicization within the armed forces had placed on top positions only the "trusted" senior officers. Many of them, with over–extended terms were finally retired, clearing the way for the promotion of deserving younger officers. Farolan was soon succeeded by Sotelo.

The organizational restructuring that resulted brought a profound change for the 15th SW. It turned into a strike dedicated unit and absorbed the 240th Composite Wing in 1987 and took control of Sangley Air Base. In exchange, it turned over the S–76 equipped 50th ARS to the 205th Helicopter Wing. At the forefront of the war effort, the unit deployed 26 T–28Ds, 12 SF 260WPs along the remaining AUH–76s. By 1988 only five AUH–76s were airworthy which led to the remaining VIP and SAR versions being fitted as gunships. Also in 1987, the HU–16s were retired from the 15th SW. Two N–22s from the 240th Composite Wing served with the 601st Liaison Squadron in support of the attack aircraft various detachments. The PhAF was less successful in acquiring new equipment that arrived only in a trickle. Ten additional UH–1Hs were supplied in 1987; some 60 airframes were in service by 1988 though many were not operational.

A patrol from 7SCR equipped with an Israeli made 5.56mm rifle Galil–SAR and a Ultimax–100. A number of Galils were imported in the 1980s as part of the internal AFP political infighting before the fall of the Marcos government. The remaining stock of Galils became a status symbol for officers in elite units.

Politicization of the AFP, however, had not been completely undone. From 1986 to 1990, rightist military factions, wary that the government of President Corazon Aquino had become "too soft" on Communists, attempted a series of coups. Without adequate civilian and military backing, however, they consistently failed to topple the newly restored democracy.

The poor security situation led to the rise of armed bands in rural areas. (via Albert Grandolini)

SAF commandos deploy in Manila. (via Albert Grandolini)

CHAPTER 5
COUNTING COUPS

Almost as soon as Marcos was out of power tensions grew in the new government. Enrile and other senior military commanders were in opposition to the leftist political officials in the Aquino government. Military officers fell out with the new Aquino regime for multiple reasons including the perceived loss of privilege and the feeling the new regime was taking too soft of an approach towards the insurgents. Aquino attempted to offer amnesty to insurgents and offer self–rule in the south along with legalizing the communist party provided they renounced violence.

Aquino was forced to harden her stance against the Communists as the military began to push for a harder line, human rights activists were dismissed from Aquino's cabinet. Despite her concessions military officers began to plan to overthrow Aquino. Inside her cabinet, General Enrile was linked was to coup attempts against the government. Aquino dissolved her own cabinet which removing Enrile as her Minister of Defense. This opened the way for Enrile loyalists to begin plotting to overthrow her government.

A coup attempt in August 1987 led to the deployment of the PhAF to suppress the military rebel. Insurgents under the command of a Colonel Honasan took Camp Aguinaldo and spread out across Manila. Drawing on RAM contacts and his own position at Fort Magsaysay,

Honasan made use of the 14th, 16th and 62nd IB, elements of the 710th Special Operations Wing, and the 6th and 7th SRC along with elements from the Light Armour Brigade that joined the insurgents during the battle.

Considerable forces remained loyal including the PC and elements of the PhAF. General Sotelo ordered the 15th SW into action. Two T–28Ds of the 15th SW, regarded as posing less risk of collateral damage then jets, conducted air strikes on rebel forces in Camp Aguinaldo. Marines in the south were readied for deployment to Manila to support the government, but the speed of the C–130s prevented them from being moved quickly.

The air strikes caused no physical damage to the insurgents, one bomb hitting the EDSA Boulevard while another landed in a civilian neighbourhood. As the PhAF remained loyal the government had access to both air strikes and mobility assets. The camp fell fast as the troops turned to the side of the insurgents. The insurgents then captured the outskirts of Villamor Air Base to prevent any planes from taking off in support of the government. Marines, the SAF, and Special Forces who stayed loyal faced them head on in defending the capital. The SAF retook a radio station the rebels had captured. Faced with the collapse of the revolt Colonel Honasan escaped on a helicopter as his

The aftermath of the F–5A strikes on the rebel T–28s. (via Albert Grandolini)

forces surrendered. The rebellion had been put down but it was not to be the last.

Post–Marcos COIN

The nation still faced a major threat by Communist insurgents, who did not lay down their weapons despite the fall of the Marcos regime. The NPA had blundered by boycotting the election of 1986, and played no role in the overthrow of Marcos. The NPA far from ceasing the rebellion with the fall of Marcos saw a chance to move into power. In December 1986 a sixty–day truce with the insurgents was agreed on between the government the NPA. The NPA sent talking points calling for the disbanding of militias, removal of the PC from COIN operations and offering talks. Talks followed, which were unpopular with hard liners on both sides. When the talks failed, Aquino scored political points, allowing the NPA to be painted as having unreasonable demands. General Illeto, founder of the Scout Rangers, was given the post of Minister of Defense. He pushed for similar tactics which had worked so well in the 1950s, small unit operations. He planned to deploy small Special Forces teams to conduct sustained operations for weeks at a time against the NPA. Ramos himself felt any offensive was to be linked with political and economic measures to undercut the message of the NPA.

The NPA actually continued to expand after the fall of Marcos, growing to an armed strength of around 25,000 by the end of 1987. The NPA was active in 60 of the nation's 73 provinces and had gained control of an estimated twenty percent of the nation's 42,000 villages. By 1986 the NPA was most active in Mindanao. The communists had set up on the island as part of a plan to tie down the government. The Mindanao front had been initially intended to be a diversion from rebel forces in Luzon, yet had grown to become the most active NPA area of operations. The Mindanao front had rebuilt since its mauling in 1975, growing to have thousands of followers. The Visaysas were another active front with northern Samar being rebel territory and Negros and Panay being actively contested.

LAD armored vehicles; a Scorpion light tank, AIFV, and M–113. Tracked vehicles have proved very useful in dealing with the rough terrain. Ongoing modernization projects have led to an increase in the number of M–113s. (via Albert Grandolini)

The NPA moved towards a limited self–reliance program, attempting to build hand grenades and shot guns. NPA made hand grenades were often more dangerous to the people using them and the shot guns, crude as they were, were reserved for the lowest status units. Primitive land mines, for attacking trucks and armoured vehicles, were built using bamboo and black powder explosives. Rebel communications also improved, radios were bought or stolen allowing the insurgents to communicate rapidly with central command. To support the larger sized units and the shift in tactics the NPA needed more money thus forcing them into greater extortion schemes against peasants, land lords and business owners in the provinces. It cost by 1988 between P40,000 and P60,000 a month to maintain an NPA company, a figure which rose to P100,000 during combat operations. The cost of keeping an NPA rebel in the field was P15 to P25 each day, which was not in the form of a salary, but in supplying food, water, soap, ammunition and cigarettes.

The AFP was over stretched, as infantry units for forced to further disperse to handle the growing NPA threat. An example was that in 1981 three infantry battalions were tasked with fighting the NPA in Cagayan, by 1988 those three battalions were dispersed across seven provinces. So despite an advantage in fire power and numbers the AFP was too scattered to mass firepower and manpower against the insurgents. Joint operations in some cases were alleged to have ended in blue on blue clashes as nervous soldiers from different services would engage each other. The regular units of the AFP fell further into a garrison mindset with units rarely venturing out of fortified base camps in anything less than platoon size, and company size operations were the standard. Operations by large units telegraphed AFP intentions and could be avoided. Occasionally larger scale search and destroy operations with PhAF support would be conducted, but the NPA would often withdraw to avoid the hammer. Units conducting operational movement on truck convoys often sat facing each other and were thus able to respond quickly to ambushes. Maintenance of weapons and vehicles was poor further limiting the amount of equipment which could be brought to bear against the insurgents. Nationwide fighting against the NPA caused the AFP to suffer a death rate of 4.4 a day up from three a day. The NPA saw weakness in the Aquino regime as the AFP itself was increasingly disloyal and the attention of the government was aimed at suppressing military insurgents.

The government was able to make use of elite units and covert operations, such as the familiar extra–judicial killings, to begin to break the insurgents. The Scout Rangers were among the most successful unit in the AFP in hunting down the NPA. A reported 95 percent of clashes involving the NPA and Scout Rangers were initiated by the Rangers. Small unit patrols and excellent training led to this feat, but the Scout Rangers were only a small part of the AFP. The Constabulary's SAF also provided the government with a force capable of conducting small unit operations; but other units were unable to match their successes.

An additional boost was in July 1987 when Aquino had the past paramilitary units disbanded and formed the Civilian Armed Forces Geographical Units (CAFGU). This new force was intended to be better trained and led and thus avoid the past allegations of corruption and brutality. The Aquino government disbanded the CHDF and then almost immediately recreated a government run militia program; the Citizens Armed Forces Geographical Units. (CAFGU). The CAFGU operated in mixed units made up 13 regular members of the AFP and 88 citizen militiamen. Typically the militiamen were equipped with older M–1 Garands. Within four years there were 89,000 CAFGUs. In Mindanao CAFGU forces accounted for seventy percent of the contacts with the NPA. To support the CAFGU program one Special Forces company as deployed in each of the military regions to provide training and leadership.

On 7 February 1987, in the village of Lupao in Nueva Ecijia the cease fire officially broke down. The AFP claimed to have clashed with a platoon sized force of insurgents. Soon it became clear something worse had occurred. A twenty–four–man patrol was engaged by an NPA ambush team, leading to the death of the leader Lieutenant Edgardo Dizon, in response the patrol rounded up and killed 17 villagers. The incident became a black eye for the Aquino regime, which was unwilling to punish the military too much and risk alienating the personnel. The men were all acquitted by a military tribunal.

On 27 February a troop train loaded with over 600 troops hit a mine on the way to Manila and was subsequently attacked by the NPA killing one and wounded four soldiers, the attack was the first in the Bicol region since the cease fire.

Alexander Nobel with rebel soldiers. (via Albert Grandolini)

PA soldiers wearing British styled DPM camouflage, adopted in the 1990s, and carrying CAR–15 rifles. The new camouflage replaced the olive drab which had been in use among PA infantry. Though the M–16A1 remained the standard infantry rifle throughout the 1990s and remains in widespread service. Via Albert Grandolini

The 5th FW deployed F–5As during fighting in late March and early April 1987 in Kalinga Apayao province against a communist training camp during the celebration of the NPA's 18th anniversary. The F–5As were suffering from lowered readiness rates as age caught up with the twenty year old airframes and this operation was a rare appearance by the F–5s. The F–5s, operating alongside attack helicopters, provided stellar service conducting air strikes in support of the 1,500 government forces involved in the operation.

Taking advantage of the disunity in the military the NPA began conducting major attacks in the Bicol region, south of Manila during the fall of 1987. The fighting in Bicol was extreme as the government worried that it might actually lose control of the province to the NPA. The NPA insurgents blew the bridges in the province, almost cutting it off from the rest of the country. This backfired as locals were angered at the major inconvenience and the local press took it as a chance to criticize the NPA. In late September a Scout Ranger battalion was flown to Bicol to support government forces, the total of Ranger battalions later grew to three and a company of Marines was flown in. Helicopter gunships supported operations against the NPA providing support as Marines and Scout Rangers took control of an NPA camp on 26 September. Additional sweeps were launched to keep the NPA off balance. In October units of the SAF were flown into Bicol to further support the AFP offensive. The major response was in no small part to reassure the local politicians, most of who supported

Aquino, that the government could protect them. Natural disaster and the fighting in Bicol hurt the NPA, as the region grew increasingly unable to support the NPA formations. The destruction caused by the NPA offensive turned much of the local population against the insurgents as prices rose and movement became difficult.

Thirty–six infantry battalions were still tied down in Mindanao along with artillery, engineers and support troops. This large investment of manpower in the south prevented the government from massing forces in the north. In Mindanao there were around six thousand NPA guerrillas, around half were well armed. Regular units of the AFP were still tied down in static defence. Often major clashes would take place only when the insurgents massed and conducted attacks on government positions.

By 1988 the Special Operations Team (SOT) concept began to bear fruit. Formerly NPA controlled villages were increasingly turned to the government side as militias would be set up under SOT control and local communist cadres captured or killed. Villages the units were deployed to were carefully chosen as the deployment went beyond North Mindanao and began to spread across the country. . The teams were central to the government's plan to win the political struggle against the NPA. Through a mix of traditional hearts and minds work coupled with interrogations and torture SOTs would identify pro–NPA elements in a community, who would typically be killed. Such tactics helped the government seize control of villages.

Another aspect of the counter insurgency campaign was the forming of vigilante gangs often under political elites. These ranged from collections of angry villagers, private militias of landowners all the way to major criminal enterprises. NPA heavy handedness in the provinces created a backlash as locals began to form private militias to fight the insurgents on their own. Over taxation and violence against suspected AFP collaborators turned many against the insurgents. Many of these groups were loosely organized as part of the Civilian Volunteer Organization (CVO). These groups operated with the tacit support of government officials and did everything from village protection to the assassination of suspected left wing organizers and strike breaking. Small arms came from the black market and through supportive government units. Clashes between vigilantes and communists took place in major cities and in rural areas. By the beginning of 1987 some two hundred vigilante gangs operated against the NPA nationwide. Unlike the CAFGUs there was no pretence of military authority over these militias.

Government operations remained lacklustre such in early 1988 when the NPA raided a PC post in the town of Bondoc in San Francisco. The rebel took the post, capturing weapons and waited in ambush for government reinforcements which didn't arrive. Fearing an ambush the AFP took four hours, moving by sea to respond rather than risk ambush travelling on the roads, and the insurgents escaped with only three killed and having captured fifteen weapons. An NPA attack on a SOT in Sipalay during April 1989, with the deaths of five soldiers, led to the launching of Operation Thunderbolt. The operation was spear headed by AUH–76 gunships and led to massive civilian dislocation, with some 30,000 being moved to an evacuation centre which soon led to the outbreak of measles and pneumonia. Despite the massive use of firepower, not a single rebel was captured and twenty–five people suspected of supporting the NPA were killed; in exchange for three hundred civilians dying in the refugee camp.

On the Moro front the Autonomous Region of Muslim Mindanao (ARMM), with its provisional capital in Cotabato City, was set up on 1 August1989 after voting was held in Mindanao.[11]

11 Initially only Lanao del Sur, Maguindanao, Sulu and Tawi-Tawi were part of the ARMM. In 2001 it as expanded to include Marawu City and Basilan.

PA troops on anti–insurgent operations. (via Lt. Colonel Dennis Eclarin)

The PA's LAD also employs the popular V–150 APC, with the machine gun turret, which is believed to have better off road mobility then the newer Simba APCs. (via Albert Grandolini)

Seven Days that Shook the Nation

Additional military coups attempts threatened the Government, but none came as close to achieving this aim as the coup from 1 December 1989 against President Aquino. It was started by an attack by MBLT4 with the support of LVTP–5 and V–150 armour vehicles which quickly smashed their way into the Villamor AB, quickly bringing it under control, seizing a dozen of UH–1Hs. The 15th SW also sided with the rebellion and began to conduct air strikes in support of the rebel army and Marine units. The loyalist positions in Camp Crane were attacked by the AUH–76s and T–28s. Three rebel T–28s also struck Malacanang Palace. The same flight of T–28s also attacked the home of General De Villa; while a lone AUH–76 hit Camp Aquinaldo. The defection on the 15th SW caught the PhAF and nation off guard. The Government ordered the T–33s of the 9th Training Squadron to fly CAPs to attempt to ward away the T–28s but by the time they were in the air the insurgents had already left. Subsequently the F–5As were ordered to fly CAPs to protect Malacanang Palace and Basa AFB. The F–5 pilots closed in the rebel T–28Ds but did not want to shoot it down over the city because of the risk of killing civilians on the ground along fellow pilots. One F–5 fired a warning shot which made the T–28Ds withdraw.

A force of around 400 rebel soldiers also captured Matcan AFB in support of the insurgents. They planned little part in the fighting and surrendered in the end with little resistance to soldiers drawn from neighbouring units. President Arroyo requested help from the United States. During the afternoon two USAF F–4Es, from the USAF 3rd TFW based out of Clark AFB, did a high–speed pass over Manila in

A PA V–150 APC, equipped with an one–metre turret armed with a 12.7mm heavy machine gun and a 7.62 GPMG, supporting a Scout Ranger unit in operations against Moro separatists in 2005. (via Lt. Colonel Dennis Eclarin)

a show of support for the government but took no directly offensive action. The planes were also useful in keeping the rebel T–28s from the skies.

The 5th FW was ordered to strike Sangley AB. The first strike was unsuccessful, as the three dispatched F–5s did not fire. On a subsequent strike F–5As launched rockets but intentionally missed their targets,. Eventually the 5th FW Commander was able to convince his pilots to take out the T–28s on the ground. Three F–5As took off, led by Major Atienza, armed only with 20mm canons so to damage but, if possible, not destroy the planes there. Eventually, their strikes knocked out seven T–28Ds and one AUH–76, and destroyed the local fuel depot. Major Atienza was subsequently awarded a Medal of Valour for his bravery during its attack. The remaining rebel AUH–76 at Sangley was flown out by its pilot, Lieutenant Gregor Mendel Panelo, to a field where he left the helicopter and fled on foot. By the end of the day the Government managed to re–establish air supremacy over Manila.

On the morning of 2 December, the 5th FW was ordered to strike the rebel forces and their armors near Camp Aguinaldo. The F–5As employed 70mm rockets, hitting their objective, but injuring also several loyal troops. Meanwhile, the PhAF deployed the AUH–76s that stayed loyal to the government to attack insurgents. As the government retook the ground, the Scout Rangers left Camp Bonifacio and redeployed to the Makati financial district to make a last stand. The Marine simultaneously pull out of Villamor AB but not before smashing the windshields of the captured UH–1Hs as to make them

A Marine Recon team posing in front of V–150 APCs. (via Timawa)

useless to the government. The insurgents also destroyed two BN–2s on the ground at Sangley AFB.

On the following morning, the Marines in Camp Aguinaldo were forced to surrender. The coup was subsequently declared for over, but the Rangers were still holding and there was sporadic sniper–fire inside Manila. It took three more days of fighting and negotiations to reduce the last rebellious elements. Overall, however, the coup–plotters had come very close to winning.

A Scout Ranger equipped with the Australian made 5.56mm F–88 carbine, a locally made variant of the Austrian AUG. The F–88s were received in small numbers and carrying such rare weapons is often a mark of status among elite units. (via Lt. Colonel Dennis Eclarin)

CHAPTER 6
NEVER–ENDING WARS

The 1990s brought no significant change of the internal situation of the Philippines, with continuing rebellions and coup attempts. The end of the Cold War brought many changes for the Philippines. The United States didn't see the country as central to their strategy in the Far East. Furthermore, its chronic instability made Washington unease to continue to be involved there. Another step in the US withdrawal occurred on 16 September 1991 when the Philippine Senate repudiated the Military Base Agreement forcing their closure. The US military finale departure signified also for the AFP the end of a secure source of funding and low cost equipment acquisitions.

The 5th Fighter Wing deployed F–5As during fighting in late March and early April 1987 in Kalinga Apayao province against a communist training camp during the celebration of the NPA's eighteenth anniversary. The F–5As were suffering from lowered readiness rates as age caught up with the twenty–year–old airframes and this operation was a rare appearance by the F–5s. The F–5s, operating alongside attack helicopters, provided stellar service conducting air strikes in support of the 1,500 government forces involved in the operation. In OPLAN Thunderbolt a large force of AFP troops conducted a search and destroy operation which displaced around 35,000 civilians. Similar large scale operations involving massed firepower between 1986 and 1991 led to 1.2 million internally displaced people.

In 1990, Colonel Alexander Nobel, the former commander of the Presidential Security Guard defected to Northern Mindanao aboard an AUH–76, joining the local insurgents. He brought alongside two additional UH–1Hs and some troops. They seized Butuan and Cagayan de Oro, without bloodshed in the seventh major coup attempt against Aquino. The Government reacted quickly. The PhAF dispatched two T–28Ds to attack the insurgents in Butuan, destroying buildings and logistics vehicles. The AUH–76 was destroyed on the ground by rockets on 4 October but one of the T–28s crashed on the way back to base the same day. The two UH–1Hs that went to the rebel side were found intact. The coup quickly ended and Noble was jailed.

In 1991 Lambat Bitag II was launched. The program was aimed to further weaken the NPA. PNP units took a more active role in COIN operations and it was hoped that such actions could be eventually passed off to the PNP entirely. The handing off of COIN duties to the PNP was premature as the organization was going through growing pains and lacked the firepower and mobility of the AFP. When President Aquino left office the number of insurgents had declined at the price of expanding provincial militias and the virtual amnesty of martial law officials. By 1992 the NPA was believed by the AFP to have 13,000 men under arms and was in control of 2,910 villages. During the decade a mix of extra–judicial killings, AFP pressure, amnesty for members and a somewhat improved economy took its toll on the NPA and membership dropped.

A well–armed Scout Ranger patrol carrying one of the handful of Ultimax–100 light machine guns in AFP usage. Small patrols drawn from the SRR typically operate as a vanguard for major operations and on separate missions aimed at collecting intelligence and conducting direct action raids against insurgents. (via Lt. Colonel Dennis Eclarin)

The Moro insurgents suffered from considerable divisions between the MILF, MNLF, and smaller more radical factions. The MILF expanded from around 6,000 in the early part of the decade to around 15,000 by the end of the decade. The MNLF's autonomous rule in the ARMM was mired in corruption and inefficiency. Nur Misauri's popularity sank. In addition, clashes took place between the AFP and elements of the MNLF and MILF. There was friction both from inside its ranks and from local political elites and pro–government factions who did not wish to end the conflict on those terms. There were numerous terrorist bombings in the south as Militant groups began to form in the Southern Philippine from veterans of the war in Afghanistan and disaffected insurgents. Darkly in Zamboanga City in 1996 PNP investigators analysed a group of these terrorist bombings and linked them to individuals linked to the AFP and the Marcos regime who were opposed to peace. Placed in context those were a minority of the total attacks but did serve to fan the flames of resentment and conspiracy theories.

The AFP and the Marines in particular were linked to nurturing of a small radical group of Islamists n Basilan Island, the Abu Sayyaf Group (ASG). This small group received arms and money to help it counteract the influence of the MNLF on Basilan and soon had over one well armed hundred members. Most of the early members were ex–MNLF and the organization soon controlled much of the island of Basilan. The group under Abdurajak Janjalani and Edwin Angeles, a long time AFP intelligence asset, soon took on a life of its own. Initially they operated alongside the Marines in various illegal activities such as illegal logging but soon took part in more lucrative kidnapping

for ransom and terrorist bombings. There were early allegations that the ASG was behind terrorist bombings against foreign Christians in Zambangao and Davao, with the AFP claiming the ASG had conducted 102 terrorist attacks from 1991 to 1995 and already had 11 camps.

There were early links between Al Qaeda and the ASG, Janjalani was in contact with Osama bin Laden's brother in law, Jamal Mohammad Khalifa, who operated charities Zamboanga City and some members received training from Ramzi Yousef. Despite the contacts with global terrorism the ASG quickly became a criminal organization which made use of terrorism.

The most ferocious new group that appeared at around this time was the so–called "Abu–Sayyaf" cell. It became infamous for its raid on the town of Ipil in April 1995. Two hundred guerrillas, moving by truck and speedboats, occupied the city, executed 53 men, women and children, robbed all the banks and larger shops, and seized thirteen people as hostages. Within a few hours after the attack about 100 insurgents were pursued by two battalions of the PA 102nd Brigade, through the forests of the province Zamboanga Del Norte. The second part of the militants fled sea to the neighbouring island, where they were placed under heavy attacks of two OV–10s. The hunt continued which mobilized four warships, two additional OV–10s, and nine MD–520s. The deployed forces became involved in a twenty–six–days–long running battle. Eventually, on 26 April 26th, the Government reported that 52 out of 56 involved Islamists were killed in Zamboanga, including their Pakistani–trained leader.

The OV–10 took over the CAS role from the T–28s and is the backbone of the fixed wing strike force despite their declining numbers. They are armed with 250lb and 500lb bombs, 70mm unguided rockets, locally designed 20mm gun–pods, and locally made cluster bombs. American support has seen the planes recently make limited use of guided bombs. Via Albert Grandolini

The MD–520 gunships surprised an additional group of militants and killed of them.

Faced with a new threat of terrorism the AFP/PNP took steps to break the terrorist networks. The PNP worked with Edwin Angeles, the man who had helped found the ASG, to root out suspected militants in and around Metro Manila. With PNP help Angeles formed his own pseudo–terrorist group and established contacts with the ASG in the hopes of capturing their leader. In December 1998 the 39–year–old Janjalani was killed in a clash with the PNP at Lamitan, Basilan. In response an ASG murdered Angeles outside of a Mosque on Isabela Balisan.

With the death of Janjalani control of the ASG went to his more violent subordinates. The main faction was under Khdaffy Janjalani and was located on Basilan. The Sulu based faction was under the leadership of Ghalid Andang, more popularly known as Commander Robot. Commander Robot led a kidnapping raid at the Sipadan resort in Malaysia. Not to be outdone the Basilan faction captured twenty hostages on Palawan including Martin and Gracia Burham. These raids were launched by speed boats and involved heavily armed bands attacking civilian targets.

Philippine Ground Units 1990–2010

Through the 1990s and early 2002s, the Philippine Army maintained a force of ten infantry divisions, one Light Armour Division (later renamed the Mechanized Infantry Division), combat support units and a robust special operations force. Around 83,200 soldiers, policemen and militiamen were stationed on Mindanao, close to 40 percent of the AFP. Battalions are assigned within an area of operations and work alongside the PNP and CAFGU to conduct patrols and other COIN operations. In 1998 under Executive Order 110, the AFP retook its primary COIN role and the PNP became a supportive agency.

The largely un–motorized units still lacked the ability to rapidly respond to emergencies. Foreign observers commented about the weak NCO cadre, corruption in the officer corps, and unaggressive leadership in regular infantry units, and poor tactical *reconnaissance* by infantry units. This would lead to small militant bands being able to outmanoeuvre AFP conventional units and escape from cordons. The Philippine army as a service was increasingly staffed by aging personnel. The poor economy led to men remaining in the service into the forties, leading to the problem of men being a lot older then they would be in western militaries or the insurgents.

The CAFGU saw an expansion going from around 37,000 in 1994 to around 61,000 by 2007. Between three thousand to ten thousand were assigned under each infantry division depending on the area. Starting in 1997, a large group of Moro fighters numbering 7,500 men were trained and organized into infantry battalions as part of the army. Many of these men were related to insurgents.

Limited improvements occurred in the ground units of the AFP during the 1990s. Despite the addition of new equipment, the army remained territorial in disposition, excluding elite units. Armoured units were deployed piecemeal as was the artillery, operating in support of local units. The majority of PA equipment remained Vietnam War vintage, with excess equipment cascaded down from the US. The same short comings remained in terms of mobility, as the army was still foot mobile light infantry. American assistance post 9/11 focused on increasing the capabilities of small units. American advisers worked with regular units to improve small unit tactics. More modern rifles, bullet proof vests, night vision goggles, and communication equipment were supplied by the US.

PA Armoured Units remained primarily a mix of wheeled and tracked armoured personnel carriers with a handful of remaining FV–101 Scorpion–76 tracked *reconnaissance* vehicles acting as surrogate tanks. Army mobility was improved with the arrival of the first of 150 Simba armoured personnel carriers from England starting in 1993. One hundred and forty–three of these were locally assembled. Armoured units are typically broken up and sent in company sized units to support Army task forces. Though few vehicles mount anything heavier than a 12.7mm machine gun.

The Philippine Marine Corps primarily conducts ground operations as part of the campaign against the Moro insurgents. Currently the PMC has 12 battalions of which three are typically assigned to the three Marine Brigades. Similar to the USMC the PMC maintains a robust Scout Sniper force. The PMC also maintains and Assault Armour Battalion which contains 90mm and APC versions of the V–300 (around twenty operational), APC versions of the V–150 (around 18 operational) and the 105mm howitzer armed LTVH–6A1 (around four operational). The Marine Corps ordered 24 V–300 in 1992, 12 with 90mm cannons and personnel carriers. The LVTH–6A1s were brought back in service and during the mid–2000s but have not served in the COIN campaign and are instead assigned to the Philippine Marine Ready Force (PMRF), alongside antiaircraft equipment and functions in a counter coup role.

The Marines began force improvements on their battalions on the model of the MBLT6. MBLT6 possessed superior tactical mobility compared to other units, because of the possession of 15 liaison vehicles and a pump boat, on the same funding as other units which often had eight vehicles. While far from totally motorized, the unit was still able to manoeuvre sub units quicker to respond to and exploit unfolding situations. Route marches were conducted with trucks attached temporaly to move the unit, as was common across the AFP. Interestingly the battalion also included a locally armoured M–35 truck and Humvee.[12] The M–35 gun–truck was used for convoy work often teamed with a V–150. The Humvee, a cargo model, was also locally armoured. MBLT6 also included a Scout Sniper team and an urban warfare/hostage rescue team, enabling limited counter terrorism operations. The units were grouped into a Special Operations Platoon under the battalion headquarters. The special operations platoon concept passed onto other Marine battalions greatly increasing their capability. The battalions operate as Marine Battalion Landing Teams (MBLT) and are typically reinforced with supporting assets such as artillery, light armour and Force *Reconnaissance* troops.[13] Marines increased in capability, while their parent service declined in capability.

The Philippine Navy languished over the decade from its high point in 1975. The fleet had not kept up regionally and was not capable enough to handle the operations required of it. The largest ship in the 1990s was the sole remaining Cannon class frigate, the BRP Rajah Humabon, which was completely obsolete, dating from the Second World War and was one of the oldest surface combatants in the world. The Rajah Humabon was supported by the Second World War vintage Corvettes; the two Auks and six PCEs. The PCEs were upgraded and refitted during the 1990s. The bright spot for the PN during the 1990s was the acquisition of three Peacock patrol corvettes and two Besson landing ships. The 76mm armed Peacocks had been part of the British Hong Kong Fleet, and while they lacked missile capability they were at least more capable of handling rough seas then much of the remainder of the fleet. The Besson were landing ships supplied by the United States, which served alongside the remaining Second World War vintage LSTs. From South Korea came six Sea Dolphins and 12 Sea Killer patrol boats, supplied at friendship prices, which reinforced the fast boat force. In 2011 the PN received a major boost with the acquisition the first of two ex–US Coast Guard Hamilton Class Cutters, which are now the largest combatant in the fleet.

2nd SRB soldiers relaxing in a former MILF camp. The Scout Rangers and Force Recon were initially misused as shock infantry during the early phases of operation, but later were employed in roles which better suited their specialist skills such as flanking dug in MILF positions through jungle marches, scouting and sniping. (via Lt. Colonel Dennis Eclarin)

The PNP deploys considerable forces to the campaigns. Provincial Mobile Groups (PMG) and Regional Mobile Groups (RMG) deploy lightly armed units to the countryside and urban areas to hold fixed positions and conduct short duration patrols. The NPA has taken to targeting police stations and capturing the M–16s carried by police officers as office often give up with little fighting, prompting some calls to remove automatic weapons all together. The elite of the PNP remained the SAF which maintains a strength of four battalions, and has an small force of V–150s in support.

Father of the Sword.

Janjalani was only loosely the leader of the ASG, he had to deal with highly autonomous commanders and the influx of millions of dollars. His focused was reported to be more on an urban terrorism campaign as opposed to other leaders who were increasingly more interested in ransoms. Janjalani tried to reach out to other Islamist militant groups to develop expertise in bomb making, including the MILF.

A former MNLF member Aldam Tilao, nicknamed Abu Sabaya, though not the formal leader, was a highly influential member of the group. Unlike Janjalani he made no pretext of upholding Koranic military values. Janjalani and Sabaya launched a series of kidnap for ransom raids. Hostages taken by the men contrasted their behaviour, believing Sabaya to be far more brutal. Sabaya was thought to be the true battlefield commander and planner of major operations. In interviews given to the media he issued threats against the militants and disparaged the capabilities of the AFP and later the Americans. Radullan Sahiron was believed to be the planner of the raid into Sipadan in Malaysia. Commander Robot made himself into a minor media sensation with his willingness to grant interviews and issue video tapes, which put him high on the wanted list.

The weakness of government control in the Southern Philippines has led to another group setting up camps in the Philippines, Jemaah Islamiyah (JI). This Indonesian terrorist group is al–Qaeda linked and its goal is a pan Islamic state from Thailand to the Southern Philippines. JI has launched dozens of operations the most infamous of which would be the bombings in Bali which killed hundreds of civilians on the resort island of Bali. JI set up camp under the protection of Moro groups and have benefited from training with the ASG and MILF and gaining experience in operations against the Philippines. They have been reported there as far back as 1995 when camps were opened in MILF territory by Indonesian veterans of the Afghan war. JI reportedly has provided bomb making skills to the Abu Sayyaf in return for the protection. Tools like cell phone bombs have been captured and JI members have been seen by hostages dating back to 2003.

In late August 2000 the Abu Sayyaf freed six hostages, for a six–million–dollar ransom. The ransom was paid by Libya, a long–time

---

12 The armour was taken from derelict LVTP-5s and LVTH-6s.

13 The Force Reconnaissance Battalion is made up of four Recon Companies (61, 62, 63, 64) and conducts reconnaissance operations as well as direct action mission.

The V-300s 90mm low pressure cannon proved among the most effective vehicle mounted weapons during the 2000 fighting. Its short barrel allowed it to maneuver through the close terrain which would have hampered other vehicles. The handful of V-300s provided considerably more firepower then the bulk of AFVs deployed in support of the operation, most of which carried only a 12.7mm machine gun. Via Timawa.

Moro insurgents with M-16 assault rifles. (via Lt. Colonel Dennis Eclarin)

supporter of the Moro insurgents. Flush with kidnap money the ASG was able to expand its size, equipment and scope of operations. By 2001 the ASG was estimated to have around 800 members, many of whom were ex-MNLF/MILF insurgents. Some ASG commanders could call on dozens of men, others less than ten. The ASG rarely sought clashes with the AFP and would break off contact if caught, unless they had suffered causalities in which case they would evacuate their wounded and dead if possible. During ambushes on AFP units the ASG could be very aggressive. They often sought to move in close to avoid air strikes and artillery, grabbing to proverbial belt buckle. Often times they would out gun similar sized AFP patrols and were able to quickly reinforce units with MILF/MNLF members and outnumber AFP patrols. Tribal and political ties and proximity of AFP units to rebel camps often led to MNLF/MILF joining in attacks against the AFP.

PhAF 1990- 2014

Because of economic problems the PhAF had to seriously curtail its development plans. Its new commander in chief, Major General Jose de Leon, had the difficult task to fulfill and fund both the needs to maintain a credible defense against external threats against the country as well as developing the COIN assets against the guerrilla groups. He formulated a five-year plan for this effect. It was tightly tailored to the available funding. Seven T-33s were supplied in 1988 as aid from the United States for the last time. Four additional F-5As were received from Taiwan in 1989. Six C-130s remained in service. Ten additional UH-1Hs were supplied in 1987; some 60 airframes were in service by 1988. However, the most pressing need was the sustaining of the 15th SW which continued to bear the main effort in combat operations. It received a major boost with new equipment to replace the worn-out T-28s, of which only a few remained combat capable. Twenty-four second hand North American Rockwell OV-10A Broncos were purchased in 1991. They augmented and later replaced the exhausted T-28Ds and took over the role of providing fixed wing support for the ground troops. With the arrival of the OV-10s the surviving T-28s were transferred to the 17th AS while the OV-10As were assigned to the 16th AS until enough entered service to replace the T-28s definitely in July 1992. In April 1992 the Philippines armed forces launched a new offensive against the insurgents on Luzon. The Special Forces located several communist bases in the Cagayan area. But the PhAF suffered quite some losses during the fighting there, having several helicopters shot down. On May 8th an AUH-76 was

Marine Scout Sniper equipped with M-95 12.7mm anti-material rifle. The rifle first saw service in the 2000 fighting and was a success, though its distinctive sound alerted insurgents to its presence on some occasions drawing suppressive fire. Via Timawa

hit by small arms fire directly over its base in Camp Adduro, and a second helicopter of the same type was lost on November 5th 1992, near Cagayan, together with an OV-10A that operated out of Cava Yan AB, and two OV-10As destroyed on the ground by NPA sappers.

In addition, 32 MD-520MG light attack helicopters were supplied in October 1990. They equipped a new squadron; the 18th Tactical Air Support Squadron. Within a few months, they were deployed against NPA insurgents in Abra. By 1996 the 20th ACS, by then renamed the

Marine Force Recon operators displaying a Marine Scout Sniper Rifle (MSSR) and an M–16A2/M–203. The MSSR saw heavy service in the 2000 fighting. The MSSR is a sniper rifle based on the M–16. As most of the engagements are fought in close terrain the MSSR's light 5.56mm round is not felt to be at a disadvantage, more so its report is similar to other 5.56mm rifles not drawing the same attention as the M–95. Via Timawa

A group of 2nd SRB officers posing at the former MILF camp Abubakar. (via Lt. Colonel Dennis Eclarin)

An M–113 of the 3rd Mechanized Infantry Battalion of the Light Armoured Division fitted with a gun–shield for its M–2 heavy machinegun. (Author's collection)

20th Attack Squadron, replaced its AUH–76s with MD–520s as well. The surviving S–76s and AUH–76s were transferred to SAR and VIP missions. Additional UH–1Hs were supplied to make up for severe attrition in the fleet, with ten entering service between 1992 and 1993, bringing the number up to 52. Of that number many were, however, not operational from spare parts issues. Six Bell 412SPs were added to the Huey fleet in 1994. Four additional BO–105s were also assembled locally between 1989 and 1992. The transport fleet was slightly improved when two C–130Bs were bought from the USAF surplus.

From Italy came 18 SIAI S–211s. The first aircraft were delivered to the 105th Training Squadron of the 100th Training Wing in 1990. They served as advanced trainer as well as a ground attack platform. A second batch of six was delivered in March 1995. The S–211 reequipped the 7th FS at Basa since that unit had retired its Crusaders.[14] The 5th FW operational rate had plummeted despite this last addition. The remaining F–5s suffered from problems of overstresses and corrosion; pilots were warned to avoid high G–load maneuvers. In the early 1990s only around two F–5As on average were in good enough shape to be called marginally combat ready. Philippines then turned toward

friendly Asian nations for help.[15] By 1997 there were only eight F–5A/Bs, eighteen S–211s, eighteen OV–10s, twenty–six MD–520s, and three C–130s operational.

In February 2001, the commander of the PhAF approved a program to turn the SF–260TPs into combat planes. The fleet of SF–260s was grounded until February 2001, when a program was initiated to bring them all into flying condition and were placed service with the newly reactivated 17th Attack Squadron (17th AS) of the 15th SW. The 17th AS had been deactivated in 1998 due to a shortage of combat airplanes. The addition of the extra airframes quickly paid off for the 15th SW. Two Blue Horizon UAVs were also acquired from Israel via Singapore in 2001 to improve *reconnaissance* in support of Army operations.

By 2003, the 15th SW had around 18 MD–520s, eight OV–10s and seven SF–260TPs in service. This small force was unable to be everywhere at once; two of the OV–10s were on Palawan,[16] two were in Zamboanga City and the other three were stationed in Cagayan de Oro City providing air support for Central Mindanao. The need for additional airframes prompted the PhAF purchase Thailand's ten remaining OV–10s. In July 2004 the 25th Attack Squadron of the 15th SW was reformed and dubbed the 25th Composite Attack Squadron, based out of Zamboanga City. The Squadron was assigned OV–10s, SF–260s and MD–520s and is tasked with providing support on operations in Mindanao. The MD–520s were also tested with forward–looking infrared (FLIR) technology to allow night operations. Night

14 For budgetary reasons, all flights on the F–8Hs had been suspended in January 1988. It was hoped that the operations would resume if funds would allow it. In fact, stored outside, the airframes were irremediably damaged by the ashes released by the Pinatubo volcano eruption of April 1991.

15 South Korea supplied thirteen F–5As between 1996 and 1998 and Jordan provided two F–5As in 1996..

16 The two plane detachment was assigned for operations over the Spartly Islands, conducting day time patrols, making up for the short fall in patrol planes.

raining was conducted with the aid of the 6th Special Operations Squadron of the United States Air Force.

The 3rd Air Division is in control of air operations against the Moro insurgents and militants and overseas five Tactical Operations Groups (TOG): TOG–9, TOG–10, TOG–11, TOG–12 and TOG–Sanga–Sanga. Each TOG is assigned, at a minimum, a detachment from the 15th Strike Wing and 205th Tactical Helicopter Wing, along with base support units. Additional assets can be attached as needed to support major operations. TOG's also supply ground based forward air controllers (FACs) to ground units. FACs have also been deployed on board helicopters to better support coordination. To maximize effectiveness, the 15th Strike Wing relied on combining fixed and rotary wing assets on air strikes. The most common combination is pairs of OV–10s and MD–520s operating together. Both planes have excellent vision for the pilots and can provide reasonable firepower against the lightly armed terrorists. The S–76 fleet, originally used as gunships, has once again been used in the attack role; not for CAS but to protect off shore oil facilities. In 2014 the PhAF began to take delivery of AgustaWestland AW–109E armed helicopters.

By 2005 fifty UH–1Hs were operational with the arrival of ones from Singapore, up from between 20 to 28 operational several years prior. The 20 UH–1Hs delivered from Singapore, came equipped for night operations. Towards the end of the decade around fifty UH–1s were operational out of eight–five in service. The PhAF took possession of seven ex–Luftwaffe UH–1Ds out of a tender for 21, before the deal with the American supplier was cancelled over alleged irregularities and delivery issues. . The PhAF's limited transport capability was provided by the 220th Airlift Wing with three C–130, and few F–27s

and a single N–22, recently this small force was augmented by two additional C–130s and two newly delivered IPTN NC–212 Aviocar.

In April 2005 the air defense command was disbanded. With the five remaining F–5s grounded the command had no capability and was a drain on resources. The remaining F–5s were retired after three decades of service, on 29 September 2005, having been grounded for the preceding two years. The airframes long worn and neglected were retired without a replacement leaving only the S–211s in the 5th FW. Money used to maintain the F–5s was earmarked for the helicopter fleet. Despite this for the rest of the decade the PhAF would struggle to keep planes in the air.

Moro insurgents. (via Lt. Colonel Dennis Eclarin)

A SRR sniper team. (via Lt. Colonel Dennis Eclarin)

An M–101 belonging to the Marine's Field Artillery Battalion. Around two dozen M–101 serve alongside a similar number of M–56/14 pack howitzers and provide dependence support despite their age. (Via Timawa)

Marine with an FN–Minimi light machine gun. The FN–Minimi purchase was surrounded by allegations of corruption, and was ultimately terminated. The South Korean made K–3 light machine gun would go onto be adopted in large numbers by the AFP in its stead. (via Timawa)

All–out War: Assaulting MILF Camps

The MILF had around 6,000 armed members around 1990 and by the turn of the twenty–first century the MILF had close to 15,000 men under arms broken up into eight divisions in Mindanao with detachments of troops in Basilan, Sulu and Tawi–Tawi in addition to the Internal Security Force (ISF) which acted as a security service and guard for MILF leadership. The ISF was based out of Camp Bushra and was set to expand its power over the armed wing of the movement. Each division had a large number of "brigades" assigned to it which were typically battalion sized or smaller. The insurgents were reported to have access to 11,350 small arms. Their heaviest weapons were RPG–2s, heavy machine guns and 60mm/81mm mortars. MILF units were based in camps, which were fixed permanent locations some of which had bunkers. These were less forts than large communities. The largest camp was Camp Abubakar, a 10,000hectare complex, which housed communication equipment, agricultural sites, weapons and containing training centres. MILF gained official acknowledgement Abu Bakar early 1999, and of several more camps in the following months. Eventually around 40 would be officially inspected by the ceasefire committees and acknowledged by the government as effectively MILF territory.

The MILF used the peace talks to build its conventional capabilities. Vietnam War vintage small arms were imported from Vietnam and Cambodia. PN patrols were stepped up in late June 1999 as reports surfaced about arms deals between the MILF/ASG and the North Korean Government. Despite reports of arms shipments, the Moro weapons remained overwhelmingly American in design, excluding the locally manufactured RPG–2s. The money to be used to purchase weapons was supplied by a little known Saudi radical, Osama Bin Laden. The MILF received a reported three million dollars from the terrorist. The other major source for military equipment was from the local black market, sourced from the AFP.

The Special Operations Group of the MILF (MILF–SOG) was officially founded in 1999 and conducted terrorist attacks in support of MILF policy. Since the early 1990s the MILF received help from foreign militants such as JI in bomb making. Patta Edris, a member of this organization was the cousin of Mukmin Edris a high ranking ASG member. These ties led to JI and ASG members passing through MILF training camps, availing themselves of MILF protection and even serving alongside MILF insurgents on the front lines to develop combat experience.

In the year 2000 new fighting broke out with the ASG and the MILF. Peace talks with the MILF began to break down prompting the AFP to conduct a punitive campaign to bring the insurgents back to the peace talks. The MILF blundered strategically and attempted a fixed defense of their territory in the form of fortified camps. Three heavily reinforced AFP infantry divisions were deployed supported by two SRBs,[17] two SFBs,[18] two Light Armor Battalions (LABs),[19] and four artillery battalions. Additional infantry battalions were deployed from Luzon and the Visayas and placed under the control of the three divisions. Nine of ten MBLTs, operational in 2000, were deployed.[20] In total 33 planes were deployed, under the command of TOG 10, 11 and 12, including a detachment of four F–5s, ten MD–520s, six OV–10s and nine UH–1s. The AFP also deployed signal intelligence (SIGNIT) units who were tasked with tracking enemy radio communications. With the support of SIGNIT units the PhAF was able to track MILF communication sites and then strike them using F–5s and OV–10s. These operations saw the F–5As dropping 750lb bombs on Camp Abubakar's communication center and airstrikes against suspected MILF leadership targets.

The AFP employed brigade sized task forces with integral light armour, artillery and with attached Scout Rangers and Force Recon units in its push against the camps. The AFP initially made the

17 Elements of 2nd and 4th, SRB
18 Elements of 2nd and 7th SFB
19 2nd and 5th LAB
20 The 1st Marine Brigade assigned to the operation had MBLT1, MBLT4, MBLT10, the 73rd Light Armored Company along with support units, artillery, Special Forces and headquarters. The 3rd Marine Brigade was assigned MBLT2, MBLT6 and MBT9.

LRR commandos wearing modern body armors and equipped with M–4 Carbines mounting reflect sights. Thanks to American support this unit carried the most advanced small arms, communication equipment and other personal gear. There were some early criticisms that the commandos were too overloaded for operations in the rugged mountains were the insurgents often operated. (via Timawa)

A Philippine Army M–60 machine gun team. (via Lt. Colonel Dennis Eclarin)

Scout Ranger carrying a short barreled M–4 carbine mounting a vertical foregrip, reflex sight, and laser aiming device. (via Lt. Colonel Dennis Eclarin)

mistake of using Scout Rangers and Force Recon units to spearhead frontal assaults on insurgent defenses which led to those units taking unnecessary losses. More flexible usage of elite units saw elements of the SRBs, MBLTs, and FRB outflanking MILF positions and forcing the insurgents to retreat. The light armour proved its use in providing close support to ground troops but the vehicles, wheeled and tracked, proved vulnerable to the rebel RPG–2s and most lacked the ability to destroy insurgent bunkers though with heavy machine gun fire positions could be suppressed. Troops learned not to keep too close to the APCs, lest they draw fire, and the APCs themselves used fire and maneuver tactics to suppress and destroy enemy positions. Additionally, engineering equipment was lacking and CAFGU members with their civilian construction equipment, protected by Rangers and Marines, were used to help clear paths for the armour to move and in a few cases chop down trees being used as sniper positions.

In a series of operations, the AFP seized Camp Omar and cleared the Carmen–Basilan base located in North Cotabato with light losses. The insurgents showed little ability to hold positions against combined arms assaults. While major assaults were going on the AFP was able to use additional forces to launch raids and aggressively patrol in contested territory to keep the insurgents off balance.

On 16 March around 700 MILF guerillas from the 303rd Brigade attacked army positions in Kauwagan, taking some four hundred

civilians hostage. Marines of MBLT1 and MBLT4 were deployed to retake Kauwagan and rescued the hostages. The MILF assault prompted President Estrada to declare "all out war" against the MILF.

Using artillery and CAS the AFP captured less well defended positions covering critical terrain and outflanked more heavily defended posts. The MILF did not defend passively and conducted counter attacks of its own which were checked through the use of heavy firepower. On 29 April the 3rd Marine Brigade pushed against Matanog to open the way for Army forces. MBLT2, MBLT6, and MBLT9 led the advance against the MILF at Matanog, which was the MILF force protecting the route to Abubakar. Hill 326 was the major MILF defensive position facing the 3rd Brigade. During the fighting at Matanog an aggressive MILF counter attack forced the elements of the 62nd Force Recon company and MBLTs to dig in and fight off the insurgents. Mortar fire along with OV–10s broke the counter attack allowing the Marines to break contact.

On 3 May 2000, the 1st Marine Brigade with MBLT4 at the head attacked MILF forces on the Narciso Ramos Highway. With the support of three OV–10s, two MD–520s, light armor and artillery the Marines were able to capture the HQ of the 4th BIAF Brigade. The 4th SRB, under TF–III Diamond, with armoured support assaulted MILF forces near Mt. Cabuago. By May 14 AFP artillery was within range of Camp Abubakar. The operation ended on 18 May, with the death

A Scout Ranger, in black, equipped with an F–88 assault rifle and a NAVSOG commando with an M–4 Carbine.. (via Timawa)

Moro insurgents on patrol. The insurgent furthest from the camera carries a locally made extended magazine for his M–16A1. (via Albert Grandolini)

A group of Special Forces Regiment operators on parade. The men wear tiger stripe camouflage which is distinct to the SFR. (via Timawa)

A Scout Ranger patrol during operations against the Abu Sayyaf band who had captured the Burnham family .The lighter equipment of the Scout Rangers, when compared to the LRC, was felt by some observers to be better suited to pursue small militant bands on foot over the rugged mountains. (via Lt. Colonel Dennis Eclarin)

of 8 soldiers and claimed 216 insurgents, and left the government in control of areas around the Narciso Ramos Highway.

The opening of the highway cleared the way to seize Camp Abubakar. The heavily reinforced 4th Division launched Operation Grand Sweeper to seize MILF positions in Masiu and Marugong to cut MILF supply lines. Once again infantry–armor task forces with CAS and artillery were able to overwhelm rebel positions Operation Grand Sweeper rolled into Operation Supreme launched by the 4th Infantry

Division aimed at seizing Camp Busrah, HQ of the 3rd BIAF Division which also functioned as a major agriculture center. Starting on 24 May the 1st Marine Brigade pushed against Camp Bushra Somiorang, the second largest MILF camp. In a fierce five day battle the Marines took the camp on 29 May.

The 3rd Marine Brigade pushed on Camp Darul Aman in Sarmiento. The camp fell to the Marines, and two MBLTs were sent to support army operations, leaving MBLT9, holding the camp. An MILF force besieged the camp, shelling and sniping at the Marine garrison. With heavy supporting fire, and the arrival of MBLT6 and MBLT7, the camp held days. With the fall of Camp Darul Aman the main camp, Abu Bakar, was open to assault.

The 15th SW supported the Marine drive to seize Camp Abubakar from the MILF. On the ground the Marines were pushed forward with close support provided by APCs and artillery. The fighting further highlighted the advantages in semi–conventional fighting of AFP against MILF defenses. The firepower of the Marines enabled them to seize heavily fortified MILF camps with moderate losses. The insurgents were unprepared for an assault on the camp and many withdrew, leaving behind weapons and documents. Camp Abubakar fell on 9 July 2000 to Marine forces as the MILF fled from the camp into the jungles. While it was celebrated by President Estrada as a major victory, with a feast of lechon (roasted pig) and beer, most of the insurgents escaped into the jungles. With the fall of their camps the insurgents began to conduct a guerilla campaign. The AFP estimated that it had reduced insurgent manpower by three percent and its weapon stocks by two percent. The campaign for all its bluster had captured insurgent camps but failed to inflict a fatal blow to the BIAF. Ominously Camp Jabal Qub, with JI members was not captured.

NAVSOG commando carrying a locally made Floro Mk.9 SMG This weapon sees minimal active service in comparison with the AR−15 family of rifles and carbines. (via Timawa)

Tactically the AFP had done well though it suffered from short comings in artillery, engineer support and armoured. Few troops had body armor or night vision equipment. Most of the armoured vehicles relied on machine guns, as there was only a limited number of V−300 with 90mm guns and 76mm equipped M−113s. The Task Forces, while operating as combined arms units, lacked the degree of artillery support militaries in the developing world would have employed in semi−conventional fighting but this proved sufficient to grind down insurgent positions and lower government losses. The AFP was also unable to make use of airmobile operations which would have allowed them to cut off fleeing insurgents. Despite these shortcomings the insurgents showed little ability to hold defensive positions and were ground down by superior firepower and maneuver. But they were far from broken military and the majority of the insurgents escaped, with their weapons.

CHAPTER 7
PURSUIT OF TERRORISTS

While the government's attention was focused on battling the ASG, terrorists increased their attacks on the civilian population, taking more hostages and bombing and raiding civilian targets. The tactics for facing the ASG were different from that which had transpired during the fighting to seize the MILF camps. The ASG did not want to give battle, and would only do so when the situation was in their favor. Thus bringing the same large scale tactics against the small terrorist bands was a tactic which did not produce much in the way of results.

The hunt for hostage Jeffery Schilling, an American held hostage, brought AFP units to Jolo in pursuit of ASG units under Commander Robot and Commander Susukan. A major offensive was launched at dawn on 16 September 2000 by AFP units moved to the island. The 15th SW assets to support the offensive conducting air strikes on suspected rebel targets. Throughout the next two weeks there was fierce fighting between Marines and the terrorists.

Two French journalists, of a total of 19 hostages, who escaped from the ASG were critical of AFP tactics. They claimed the ASG band who held them hostage had no close encounters with the AFP, but witnessed air strikes. The journalists claimed PhAF airstrikes were random, and hit civilian targets, failing to injure or kill any of the terrorists. But the constant attacks forced the ASG to continue to move allowing them to sneak away. During a major assault on the ASG, attempting to rescue their remaining seventeen hostages, two villages, Bandang and Samak were destroyed in a combined arms assault making use of airpower and artillery.

A well–armed but lightly equipped Scout Ranger unit posing next to one of the handful remaining C–130s. (via Lt. Colonel Dennis Eclarin)

The Korean made KM–450 is the standard light utility vehicle of the PA. (Author's collection)

The shortage of naval and air assets allowed the ASG to strike at will across the south. The PhAF, with assets based out of Jolo, in support of ground forces conducted multiple air strikes on insurgents, some of which were alleged to have wounded civilians. By the second week of fighting in Jolo the government forces claimed to have killed 104 terrorists. During the hunt of ASG terrorists and their hostages in Jolo during 2001 two UH–1Hs and one S–211 were deployed along with PN patrol boats. To make up for the shortage in CAS assets period several UH–1Hs were armed with forward firing machine guns, along with door guns, to support the ground operations.

On 27 May 2001 at Dos Palmas Beach Resort on the island Palawan the Abu Sayyaf conducted a major seaborne raid. Basilan based terrorists took 20 hostages, three American citizens, 14 Filipino guests and three resort employees. In response, one company of MBLT6 was airlifted to Palawan Province and joined Task Force Peacock of WESCOM. On 1 June an additional company from MBLT6 was sent to Basilan to assist in operations. The worsening situation on Basilan forced the deployment of MBLT1, MBLT3, MBLT5 and the 62nd and 63rd FR companies to the island. In 12 June 2001 Philippine–American hostage Guillermo Sibero was claimed to have been beheaded by the ASG on the 103rd anniversary of Philippine independence. The body was left to be found by government forces. The murder redoubled efforts to track the insurgents. Also an additional fifteen hostages were taken by the ASG after an attack in the village of Lantawan in Basilan.

Scout Ranger patrol moving through rough terrain. The Scout Ranger closest to the camera is carrying a 5.56mm FN–Minimi. (via Lt. Colonel Dennis Eclarin)

A small patrol of Scout Rangers is dropped by UH–1H. (Via Lt. Colonel Dennis Eclarin)

Along with more "conventional" deployments in support of COIN operations, LRR sniper teams have seen limited deployment on PhAF helicopters providing aerial support. (via Timawa)

On 26 July a police raid in Basilan captured 16 ASG militants. On 27 July an ASG camp in Jolo held by some 100 militants fell to the AFP. As the AFP attacked the camp the militants fled, leaving behind weapons and supplies but escaping. On 10 August MBLT5 and the 63rd Force Recon company clashed with a large force of ASG, claimed to have numbered ninety, in the battle the Marines claimed to have killed seven. On 22 August elements of MBLT3 and the 62nd Force Recon company clashed with a force of around one hundred ASG militants, killing commanders Imam Hapilon and Mukhtar Mingkong.

SOCOM

The Special Operations Command (SOCOM) was first established in June 1996. By the beginning of the 21st Century the Army's special operations force was built around three units, the Special Forces Regiment (SFR), Scout Ranger Regiment (SRR) and Light Reaction Battalion (LRB). SOCOM grew in importance as a function of the counter terrorism campaign and the continued COIN campaign against the NPA and dissident Moro groups. Around 5,000 personnel are assigned to SOCOM, most on deployed on operations.

Caught flat–footed by the Abu Sayyaf and their kidnap gangs the AFP took steps to counter them. Highly mobile kidnap gangs using speeds boats were difficult to track and could strike against any soft target and hit in Moro territory relying on money and local support to hide. With large numbers of troops tied down fighting the MILF main forces and the NPA, small militant bands could operate almost at will.

The PA took the step of outlining plans to create a special reaction unit for counter terrorism. The LRB was to be made up of Scout Rangers and Special Forces trained operators and supplied with top of the line equipment. The first Light Reaction Company (LRC) [21] was ready for action by the year 2000, trained in hostage rescue, strategic *reconnaissance*, and direct action missions. The LRC benefited from American aid in the spring of 2001, because several American citizens were held hostage by the ASG, and Philippine law prevented American combat units from conducting operations on Philippine soil. On 8 July 2001 the LRC was sent to the south to hunt the kidnap gangs. The formation of a combat unit, trained for hostage rescue,

21 The LRC numbered around ninety members.

marked a drastic shift from the use of either special units used ad–hoc in the role or regular units simply assaulting rebel positions, in the off chance that hostages could escape. The first combat actions of the LRC were moderately successful as during long range patrols teams made contact with the ASG, allegedly inflicted several dozen causalities. These patrols were a typical combat mission, which any AFP elite unit was able to undertake. In the operations to come LRC effectiveness would be hampered by the inherent AFP weakness of mobility and rapid response capability.

American advisors were critical of the large scale sweeps and reliance on artillery by regular army units. The Americans favored small unit intelligence driven operations employed by units like the Scout Rangers and the LRB. The Americans also remarked on other AFP weakness, near the top was a shortage of tactical and strategic mobility. The battle space the AFP was conducting operations in was massive but the military remained generally static. Units were basically territorial, tasked with operations in a given area and were scattered to provide security and had difficulties massing combat power. There were shortages in trucks, helicopters, fixed wing transports and ships. This made the AFP slow in reacting to tactical and strategic situations. The most mobile units remained the Marines and various special operations units, such as the Scout Rangers, LRB and Special Forces.

SOF led operations against the terrorist bands became a standard feature of AFP missions against the Abu Sayyaf and JI. Specializing in small unit patrolling and possessing better training and equipment

A close up on the rail mount of a K–3 SAW. (via Lt. Colonel Dennis Eclarin)

The PA has updated a battery of M–101s with a French designed barrel based on the GIAT LG–1 Mk.2. These updated howitzers have a longer range and can make use of more modern ammunition. (via Raymond Cruz)

then regular infantry units, the SOF units killed or captured the majority of the military HVTs killed and captured on operations. A controversial element of training includes the use of trainees to conduct combat operations. This would lead several times to tragic incidents of trainees being mauled by militant bands in poorly planned assaults. Politically elements of SOCOM were linked to attempts to overthrow the Arroyo government. In the aftermath of the 2003 Oakwood mutiny both the SRR and SFR were reduced to

three battalions each. Previously the Scout Rangers had nine combat battalions and the Special Forces had six combat battalions. Later the units were gradually expanded in size again as the need for elite units was clear.

By 2003 two additional LRCs finished training, bringing the unit up to a full battalion. The LRC continued its deployment style; small detachments were assigned to support AFP operations across the archipelago, focused on operations against the Moro insurgents and militants. LRCs were rotated on operations lasting normally half of a year against the militants while other units rotated back for rest and retraining, allowing a company to always be on operations against the militants. The LRB operated in a similar role to earlier operations, long range small unit patrols, raids against ASG camps and as a shock force for specific operations. The rise in helicopter availability and the priority given to their operations allowed elements of the LRB to conduct airmobile raids against ASG camps and to drop patrols off into rebel territory, but typically units were moved by truck on operational moves and patrolled on foot. In 2014 it was announced that the LRB would be brought up to a full Regiment, the Light Reaction Regiment (LRR).

The Scout Rangers remained the Army's elite COIN strike force, numbering in time four battalions of three companies each along with HQ units along with training units. [22] Functioning in their role of long range patrolling and direct action the Scout Rangers operated against the NPA and Moro insurgents/militants with great effect. Small patrols would operate as a vanguard for major operations and on separate

---

22 Scout Rangers patrols typically are seven men strong, two of which make up a squad. A Scout Ranger company is around eighty men strong.

missions aimed at collecting intelligence and conducting direct action raids against the insurgents.

Receiving far less media attention was the Special Forces Regiment (Airborne).[23] The SFR currently has six SFBs, including three river companies. Their units operated both alongside pro government militias, conducted long range patrols and raids against insurgents though they conducted direct action raids with less frequency then the SRR. Not part of the army but pivotal to the operations was the PN's Naval Special Operations Group (NAVSOG). This four–thousand–man unit[24] functions in a similar style to the United States Navy SEALs, these commandos operated on land and sea patrolling the jungles and the inner waterways and coastal seas hunting the militants. NAVSOG also conducted direct action raids against militants. The PhAF maintains the 710th Special Operations Wing, divided up into six company sized Groups of four squadrons each.[25] This eight–hundred–man unit conducts light infantry COIN operations as well as provided FACs for ground units, counter terrorism assignments.

With the decline in tactical airpower tube artillery like this WW–2 vintage M101 provide the bulk of fire support. (via Lt. Colonel Dennis Eclarin)

US Involvement and War on Terror

After the 11 September terrorist attack, the American military deployed around one thousand advisors as part of Operation Enduring Freedom (OEF), to the Philippines to help the struggle against ASG which was suspected to be tied to terrorist Osama Bin Laden. American support came in the form of money, cascaded down equipment and training. The US Special Forces advisors in the Philippines were not allowed to conduct offensive operations against the ASG but were allowed to return fire if fired upon. Under Philippine law foreign soldiers were prevented from conducting combat operations, which over the next several years would see joint training conducted in war zones.

The first US troops to arrive belonged to the Joint Task Force 510 (JTF–510), in January 2002. They were followed by signal intercept teams to track terrorist communications, MH–60 and MH–47 helicopters, P–3C Orions and C–130 Hercules transports. The all weather flying ability of the MH–47Es was vital as the UH–1s could not fly safely at night or in poor weather conditions. The Americans provided the AFP with around one hundred million dollars' worth of equipment including eight UH–1Hs, one C–130B transport, small arms, NVGs, mortars, and radios. Yet the US presence was controversial as segments of the Philippine public was opposed to allowing in the American armed forces. The US approach was in favor of small scale actions relying on intelligence and advanced technology. To complement the military approach, US Special Forces conducted their long standing hearts and minds operations. Hospitals and schools were planned to be constructed along with roads, which not only made AFP movement quicker but increased trade between villages and towns. American Special Forces trained AFP units in night actions focusing on elite units and the PhAF. Night operations were critical because the militants preferred not to fight at night, lacking night vision equipment of their own.

The governor of Basilan, Wahab Akbar, began to emulate ASG tactics in tackling the militants. His private forces would find and kill militants and kidnap their families when they kidnapped locals. Dozens of locals, suspected of supporting the militants were jailed without trial and others were simply killed. These operations went on without American support or approval, which was focused on hearts and minds of the locals.

Operation Daybreak

During the post 9–11 operations to rescue the Burnham family the 3rd Marine Brigade relied on information supplied by informants within the ASG. The Marines conducted intense patrols and often had clashes with the group yet were unable to pin them down and free the hostages. There were further reports that far from hunting the ASG group some AFP units were selling them supplies. The AFP used a media disinformation strategy to convince Sabaya that they thought he was in Basilan rather than in Zamboanga del Norte. The LRC was deployed by C–130 to Basilan. A combined force was deployed made up of Scout Rangers, the MBLT2's Recon Platoon, the LRC and NAVSOG backed with assets from two infantry battalions, the 205th HW and 15th SW and naval ships. UH–1Hs flew in several LRC teams to hunt the militants but the raiders were often late or the militants were able to break contact and escape.

On Christmas 2001 a seventy–man Scout Ranger force got into ambush positions within a few meters of the ASG but were accidentally discovered by a member of an NGO whose screams alerted the militants and in the fire fight the Abu Sayyaf hostage group was able to escape with the hostages out of the kill zone. The Marine units involved were pulled out at the start of 2002 and replaced by Army units for varied reasons. The MBLT's were officially redeployed to deal with MNLF insurgents, who had gone into open revolt, though at higher levels it was thought the Marines were taking too long in freeing the hostages and some went further suggesting collision between the Marines and the ASG militants. Misauri's revolt saw around 500 MNLF insurgents attacking pooling sites to prevent elections in the ARMM which would have ousted him. The revolt, without support of the wider MNLF, was quickly broken after some 147 deaths, and he was arrested after fleeing to Malaysia.

On 19 February two MD–520s conducted operations in support of ground forces who had been ambushed by the militants on the island of Tingulan, off the coast of Basilan. Exercises with American Special Forces were being conducted nearby, which prompted the AFP to deny that the US had any role in the clash. By May 2002 the AFP felt it had a good idea on the location of the hostages through the use of local informants. The task force was made up of the 1st SRB, a LRC and several UH–1Hs and MD–520s. Aggressive patrolling led to repeated clashes with the ASG. The Philippine Army was able to make use of local contacts to put a satellite tracking beacon into a bag of supplies given to Sabaya by locals the terrorist leader thought supportive of their cause. With the tracking beacon in place JTF–510 was able to track his movements and that of the hostages. Additionally poor field

---

23 The Regiment dropped the HDFG(A) moniker in 1989.

24 NAVSOG is divided into 11 Naval Special Operations Units, each comprising several platoons.

25 The 720, 730, 740 and 750 Combat Groups.

Masked Moro insurgent with an M–16A1/M–203 combo. (via Lt. Colonel Dennis Eclarin)

Marine mortar team with an 60mm M–2 mortar, the standard company level mortar of the AFP. (Via Raymond Cruz)

Marine 81mm mortar unit. (via Timawa)

craft, such as dropping food wrappers, allowed a thirty–seven man Scout Ranger platoon to track the militants. The LRC was unable to take part in the operation to free the Burnham family; there were no helicopters available to move them in and they were a full day's march away. On 7 July the Scout Rangers manoeuvred assaulted the camp. In the resulting fire fight two hostages were killed and one wounded. In spite of the bad weather a UH–1 was used to remove the wounded Mrs. Burnham. Seven of the ASG members escaped but AFP forces were on their tril.

Revenge on the ASG was not long in coming as Abu Sabaya, the leader of the ASG band, was found in 21 June 2002 while at sea. His pump boat was tracked by an USN P–3C and a tracking device located on the boat. The P–3 helped coordinate an intercept by elements of NAVSOG and the PMC. In the resulting fire fight near Sibuco Bay, Abu Sabaya was killed and four ASG militants were captured in the lop–sided naval engagement. Two MH–47Es were deployed to the area to illuminate the scene of the battle and help look for Sabaya's body which was never recovered. While the operation did highlight shortcomings in terms of helicopter availability the hunt also showcased the use of high tech sensors and a more aggressive SOF led hunt for the militants. Over the next several years ASG commanders were killed by SOF units. The American equipment was vital in tracking the ASG, the PhAF/PN had nothing like the P–3 or MH–47E.

Three task Forces were set up to finish the ASG.[26] As there were no more hostages the AFP had a freer hand in operations against the insurgents. The AFP put the ASG under more pressure. In June near Pitikul the commander of the 9th SRC was killed in clash with a group of Abu Sayyaf which according to the military was around one hundred strong led by Janjalani and Radulan Sahiron. The band was being tracked by Scout Rangers and American UAVs. Sahiron and Janjalani were reported to have combined their groups during the pursuit for safety in numbers, making them easier to track as well.

In August, 70 members of the LRC were deployed by air to Jolo to support the operations aimed at rescuing four hostages. Alongside the LRC was an MBLT and an SRB. During the follow up operations the units put the ASG under pressure by attacking suspected rebel camps near Patikul. By August it was claimed that the LRC had been in over 50 firefights with the ASG and suffered only two wounded in exchange for killing several of the militants. During additional battles in October several AFP troops were killed fighting the ASG in Jolo, but the AFP kept the pressure, striking the ASG at every opportunity, supported by PhAF assets and artillery. A further 11 Marines from MBLT3 were killed in an ambush by the Abu Sayyaf while attempting to rescue four kidnapped missionaries. The PA and Marines backed by artillery and the 15th SW continued to move forward and hunt the militants. The LRC deployed a platoon sized detachment to support a MBLT in hunting an Abu Sayyaf hostage group on Jolo in December.

26 Task Force Bulldog, made up of 1st SRB, the LRC, 44th IB, Task Force Jersey made up of a MBLT and Task Force Panther made up of 15 SRC and 1st IB

SOCOM operators repelling from a PhAF UH–1. (via Lt. Colonel Dennis Eclarin)

Between 9/11 and the beginning of 2003 over 300 soldiers and Marines were killed in action with the Abu Sayyaf and other rebel groups with scores more wounded

MILF Trouble

The year 2003 also marked a return large scale fighting between the Philippine Government and the MILF. The two–year cease fire broke down and clashes began. The MILF had reorganized its forces from six territorial divisions into nine more flexible Base Commands, with the 101 holding Abu Bakar. The Base Commands varied in size from several hundred to several thousand, as some were formed from former divisions and others from brigades. The new units made use of traditional camps but were to break down into smaller units and conduct guerilla warfare in response to government offensives. The 107 Base Command near Davao City was faced with the problem of a small recruiting pool relative to the area's population, while the 108th Base Command in Zamboanga was virtually autonomous due to its distance form HQ and took part in regular unauthorized looting and extorting of civilians. MILF–SOG began to operate more closely with ASG/JI for ideological and commercial reasons. This led to further breakdown of control over units and more reliance on personal relationships to keep some semblance of control.

As clashes escalated the MILF kidnapped forty civilians and were then pursued by elements of the Marines and the 6th ID who were being supported by PhAF assets. The PhAF claimed around 178 insurgents were killed by air strikes. On 11 February 2003, five AFP battalions surrounded the Camp Buliok located in Liguasan Marsh in North Cotabato. The terrain was difficult but the AFP was well prepared with aerial photographs of the camp. The AFP began to attack the camp, only to be called off by President Arroyo. Less than

a day later the on elements from the 6th ID and 1st and 2nd Marine Brigades were back in action well supported by artillery and airpower. The 200–hectare camp was captured by 15 February with the MILF admitting the loss of 47 insurgents for the loss of three government soldiers and militiamen killed and 55 wounded. During the month long clashes, an MILF–SOG attack blew up five power plants that supplied the power for Mindanao, blacking out much of the island. In March an estimated 1,000 MILF insurgents launched a counter attack to reclaim lost territory around Camp Buloik but were beaten back by the 6th IB with heavy PhAF support. The AFP claimed to have killed around 200 insurgents in this and follow up operations, a figure disputed by the MILF who claimed to have lost only sixteen. Fighting spread across North Cotabato, Sultan Kudarat, and Maguindanao, drawing in the 106th and 109th Base Commands.

In May 2003, the PhAF launched air strikes on MILF bases, suspected of housing ASG and Pentagon Gang militants. Around 120 250lb bombs were dropped on suspected bases. A MILF communications centre was bombed by two SF–260s along with two MD–520s which were followed up by an artillery barrage. The PhAF claimed to have killed as many as sixty insurgents in the camps. The destruction of Camp Gumander was hailed as a major success in preventing it from being turned into a major fortified position by the MILF. By 18 May an estimated 85 Moro insurgents had been killed by AFP units in the fighting in Lanao del Norte. A few weeks later several members of the Pentagon Gang were reported killed by Marine artillery. As was customary the MILF began to break up into smaller units and rely on hit and run tactics. The AFP deployed elements of the 54th Engineering Brigade to help build houses for the displaced ad the fighting moved on.

PA ground troops being moved by a PN landing craft. (via Lt. Colonel Dennis Eclarin)

In July 2003, during operations against ASG commander Janjalani the PhAF deployed two OV–10s, three MD–520s, and two UH–1Hs. Janjalani gathered some seventy–one militants in the Butril area when they were attacked: OV–10s dropped eight 250lb Mk.81 bombs on his suspected hideout while three MD–520s then strafed the fleeing insurgents. Khadafy Janjalani was forced to leave Jolo in July and flee to Sultan Kudarat because of the increasing military pressure on the island. It was reported in November 2003 that Janjalani moved to Basilan to avoid the increased government patrols in Sultan Kudarat. Intense government pressure, provided by local intelligence assets and aggressive patrolling, kept him on the move.

Furthur Rahman al–Ghozi a high ranking ASG commander connected to JI and AQ escaped from Camp Crame in July 2003 along with Abdul Mukim Edris and Omar Opik Lasal. On 15 October al–Ghozi was killed at an AFP checkpoint in Pigcauayan North Cotatabo under murky circumstances. On 8 December, Commander Robot was captured after a raid by commandos on his safe house in Indanan, suffering several wounds to his legs, leading to the amputation of one. AFP offensives during the preceding years reduced the ASG to around 400 militants, not all of whom were "full time." Many of the men fighting under its banner were drawn from criminal gangs and were interested in making money, not in fighting for an Islamist state. Despite the reduction in manpower, with the connection to the JI the ASG became able to conduct major terrorist attacks similar to the Bali bombing. The ASG moved to bigger scale bombing attacks as a way to strike fear such as single most murderous act the bombing of Super Ferry 14 in Manila Harbor in February 2004, an attack in which 194 civilians died. Other bomb attacks were much smaller scale affairs.

Two young Moro insurgents posing at an insurgent camp. (via Lt. Colonel Dennis Eclarin)

In late November 2004, two OV–10s and four MD–520s of the 15th SW conducted a series of bombing missions on a suspected meeting of around 50 JI and Abu Sayyaf militants, killing at least ten suspected militants. An attempt to land commandos in two UH–1Hs was forced back by small arms fire, and one was damaged. After the operation it was learned the ten dead Moros came from the MILF, threatening the tense ceasefire.

A Scout Ranger unit wearing new gear such as Kevlar helmets and vests and carrying a M–67 90mm recoilless rifle, which provides close support firepower for AFP combat units for primarily use against soft targets and enemy field positions. Recently the PA has ordered RPG–7s to replace older recoilless rifles. (via Lt. Colonel Dennis Eclarin)

Operations in January of 2005 against Janjalani relied mostly on air strikes from OV–10s and MD–520s as the terrain at the Butilam marsh in Datu Piang in Maguindanao was too swampy to rapidly deploy ground units. Due to the increased number of UH–1Hs, six helicopters were used to fly in ground troops to recover the bodies of militants and to sweep the area for surviving militants. A fierce battle broke out as the helicopters tried to land and the PhAF went into action bombing and strafing enemy positions allowing the ground forces to be flown in. An estimated fifty militants were killed in the fighting.

The close proximity of the operations to MILF zones led to a clash between MILF forces and an army patrol in January in Maguindanao province. Twenty–four people, including eight soldiers, were killed in the fighting as negotiators on both sides attempted to stop the battle. Air strikes were conducted throughout the month on MILF positions. To support army operations five UH–1s were deployed along with an eight plane detachment from the 15th SW. In late January the government claimed to have killed 40 members of the MILF, JI and the ASG in PhAF air strikes aimed at followers of Wahid Tundok, whose group killed seven soldiers.[27]

To further complicate the situation, MNLF insurgents loyal to then jailed leader Nur Misuari launched attacks on unsuspecting AFP units inflicting dozens of causalities including 16 killed. MNLF forces were estimated at five to 800 members and ASG leader Sahiron, the target of the AFP units, was reportedly part of this operation. Regular infantry, Scout Rangers, Marines and a LRC were deployed in Jolo during February to defeat the remainder of the MNLF.

Starting on 7 February AFP units assaulted MNLF positions and fought to cut off their escape routes. Forty government soldiers were wounded in the clashes with the MNLF on the 7th. Six PA/PMC battalions supported by a LRC assaulted rebel positions. Four OV–10s and four MD–520s, based out of Jolo airport, were assigned to provide CAS. An additional MBLT was moved in by sea to support

Commandos of the 710th SPOW outfitted for CT missions. The operator closed to the camera carries an MP–5 with a reflex sight, not commonly carried on counter insurgency operations in more rural areas. (via Timawa)

27 Wahid Tudndok was an MILF commander who "officially" operated outside the MILF chain of command.

MILF insurgent with a "Baby Armalite" mounting a scope. Such weapons are often captured form AFP forces or acquired on the black market. (via Lt. Colonel Dennis Eclarin)

Moro insurgents displaying their firearms. They wear the mix of camouflage uniforms and civilian clothes common to Moro insurgents. (via Albert Grandolini)

the fighting. On 10 February MNLF troops attempted to overrun a company sized unit but were repulsed by artillery and reinforcements from the AFP. The insurgents retreated to Bitan–ag, a hilltop position, which fell to AFP soldiers the same day. AFP ground units brought in mortars and heavy weapons and set up positions to close off escape routes. In seven days, 33 soldiers were killed with over 70 wounded, while 72 insurgents were reported killed. Among the dead was Lieutenant Colonel Dennis Villanueva commander of the 53rd IB. Lieutenant Colonel Villanueva died of shrapnel wounds because of limited helicopter support to evacuate the wounded. As the fighting drug on the military reduced their estimates of enemy forces to three hundred due to enemy causalities from air and ground attacks.

Scout Rangers, Marines and an LRC assaulted other MNLF positions throughout the next week. Several camps were overrun by the AFP. On February 24th the 53rd IB, with MD–520s operating in support, overran ASG positions on Budkaha Mountain, killing ten and causing a general rout as ASG militants fled in small groups.

To avoid the air strikes the MNLF fighters broke into small groups as the larger units they had grown accustomed to operating with were too easy to fix in position. UH–1Hs were used to redeploy small units around the battlefield while the small fleet of C–130s flew in soldiers and supplies to staging areas. The operations highlighted the lack of equipment among line infantry units. For example, units fighting near Silangkan had enough helmets for only half of the 60 soldiers and enough protective vests for a sixth of them. Medical support was bad as the army lacked a staffed and supplied field hospital in the area.

By massing manpower and fire support the AFP was able to systematically overwhelm MNLF forces. Commander Ibrahim was reported killed in the fighting. The clash also showed the foolishness of attempting to engage the AFP in a standing conventional operation. By the end of the fighting the AFP lost 40 members.

Heavy fighting with the Abu Sayyaf erupted in April near the Butilan marsh located in Maguindanao province. OV–10s bombed on ASG positions and in the subsequent fighting the army claimed to have killed two ASG members, though sniper fire prevented them from recovering the bodies. In August Special Forces were flown into Datu Piang were there were reports of Janjalani's presence. After aerial bombardments ground forces were moved in to sweep the area, but it was clear that he had escaped the net. The houses used by the militants had been destroyed by shelling and air strikes but the militants had escape.

Three complete LRCs were deployed around Talayan to conduct operations against the ASG and JI. The six UH–1Hs and several MD–520s were deployed in support. The operation on 15 April started with a recon squad being landed at night which ran into trouble from militants near the landing zone. Follow on units from the LRC were landed onto the landing zone which engaged the ASG as UH–1Hs

flew in supplies and more soldiers and removed the wounded. By the second day of combat the UH–1Hs removed the LRC at the cost of three members wounded and several militants killed. In May a joint 6th ID/LRB operation supported by MD–520s and UH–1Hs hunting Janjalani led to the death of five militants. The hunt was pressed with air strikes and airmobile raids onto suspected camps. PhAF and LRC succeeded in destroying encampments and killing several militants.

In July, the 1st LRC, supported by two MD–520s and two UH–1s, conducted operations at Tamar Village, near Talayan Town, after receiving information that Janjalani was in the area. They made contact with the ASG and four militants were killed and three wounded in the fighting for the loss of no government troops. The operation was cleared with the MILF, who were claimed to have provided intelligence. Several days later MILF small arms fire damaged a UH–1 near Talayan Town. The helicopters, two UH–1s transporting troops hunting the ASG, came under fire as they landed near MILF positions. In August 2005, the Special Forces operators launched a raid which killed Ismin Shairon, the son of Radullan Sahiron.

The Scout Rangers captured several camps in early November killing several militants in firefights. In response, the ASG launched mortar attacks near Panamao destroying a Mosque and several homes. In late November, an Army brigade operating under Joint Task Force Comet (JTFC) supported by two armed S–211s, two OV–10s and several MD–520s overran ASG camps on Sulu. JTFC was a combined AFP task force made up of armor, infantry, engineers, and artillery sent to hunt the Abu Sayyaf. The AFP launched the operation in hopes of killing or capturing the Radullan Sahiron. It was reported that the air strikes killed no ASG members and that the fifteen militants who died were killed in the clashes with Army troops.

Oplan Tidal Wave, created by Brigadier General Juancho Sabban, sought to increase the use of intelligence driven special operations with a simultaneous civic actions program aimed at increasing development in Moro areas. Brigadier General Sabban made use of American aid to help in development projects, such as roads, schools and health clinics. The type of operations had more in common with the Huk strategy of the 1950s then with the MNLF war of the 1970s. The Joint Special Operations Task Force Philippines (JSOTF–P) made up of US Special Forces provided intelligence support to the AFP. Support was also provided by the MILF which helped the AFP identify members of JI and the ASG. MILF members also took part in hunting down HVTs to win support from the US and help the peace talks move forward.

Scout Ranger with the new digital camouflage carrying a K–3 SAW. (via Lt. Colonel Dennis Eclarin)

A mixed group of Scout Rangers and Special Forces members. The Special Forces wear standard DPM fatigues while the Rangers wear their signature black uniforms. (via Lt. Colonel Dennis Eclarin)

A PMC V–300 vehicle crew displaying 90mm HE rounds. (Via Timawa)

In late August 2006, Southern Command was split into two to better focus operations. The command was broken into Eastern and Western Mindanao commands. Before the split Southern command had three infantry divisions, two SFBs, one LRC, Scout Rangers, Marine detachments, a PhAF TOG, two naval task forces, two joint task forces and supporting unit. Southern command had some sixty percent of AFP assets, as it faced not only the Moros but also the NPA. The division was to allow the commanders to better marshal resources. Under Operation Ultimatum, aimed finishing off the militants, five MBLTs, three battalions of the 103rd Infantry Brigade, supported by Scout Rangers and Special Forces detachments, an LRC, three divisional *reconnaissance* companies and the elements of the 710th SPOW were sent on operations.

Janjalani's Death

On 1 August 2006 a clash broke out near Patikul town, in Jolo, after reports came in on a meeting between Janjalani, Umar Petek and Dulmatin. This sighting led to more troops being brought in to hunt HVTs. Soldiers and marines backed by MD–520s attacked the militants in Marang. Two marines were wounded in the initial fighting against some 150 militants present. A reported three militants were killed in the fighting.

On 4 September six Marines, of Force Recon Class 12, were killed with another nineteen wounded in a major clash with between 150 and 200 militants. The Force Recon platoon numbered 27 me but initiated

the clash. The fact that the Marines had only three night–vision sets caused them in part to wait until first light to begin the clash. During the clash additional militants arrived and attacked the Marines. The Marines on the scene had no idea how important this clash was. MD–520s attacked the fleeing militants. In the clash a reported 70 militants were killed or wounded, in exchange for six Marines killed. In the aftermath of the fighting the Marines were withdrawn with the aid of the Joint Special Operation Task Force. On 27 December a group of ASG prisoners brought Marines to a grave in Patikul. Only later did Marines discover that Janjalani had been killed in the clash.

The year 2007 started disastrously for the militants. On 5 January Jundam Jamalul and Abu Hubaida were killed, along with four other militants, while riding on a pump boat in a clash with NAVSOG and Marines. On 9 January Binang Sali was killed in a joint SF/SR raid coordinated by Joint Task Force Comet. The Abu Sayyaf suffered a major setback as Abu Solaiman, Janjalani's deputy, was killed. On 16 January a sixty–man strike force drawn from the 8th SFC located his camp and surrounded it. The clash started in the morning as Solaiman got too close to elements of the patrol and spotted them and was shot.[28]The death of Solaiman left four major commanders on the run: Radullan Sahiron, Isnilon Hapilon, Abu Pula, and Abu Parad. On 18 January Marines battled an Abu Sayyaf band under Sahiron and Abu Pula, capturing three and killing another nine on Jolo. Oplan

---

28 Sgt. Raul Suacillo who took the fatal shot on Solaiman, won the Interim Gold Cross Medal for valor and was killed on July 3rd 2007 during a training exercise at Fort Magsaysay when the gun a trainee used was loaded with live ammunition. Sgt. Suacillo was thirty-four years old at his death.

Scout Rangers carrying M–16A1 (Enhanced). This local upgrade of the Vietnam War vintage M–16A1 refurbishes worn rifles and adds the M–16A2 style hand guard, but retain the M–16A1 barrel and receiver. (via Lt. Colonel Dennis Eclarin)

Ultimatum was extended by the AFP to continue the hunt for the ASG and JI.

Commander Malik, of the MNLF, began to clash with the AFP. He was accused of hiding the planners of the 2002 Bali bombing. Malik's forces ambushed an AFP patrol, killing two and wounding eight and mortared a Special Forces camp. His followers had broken into small groups to attack government positions and evade detection. General Hermogenes Esperon Jr., Armed Forces chief of staff, signaled that small unit patrols would phase out battalion sized sweeps on operations against them. In late April four MBLTs were assigned with "mopping up" operations.

Bloody Summer of 2007

At 4:30a.m. on 10 July 2007, a Force Recon patrol set out towards Tipo–Tipo as a vanguard for a fifty man task force drawn from elements of MBLT8 traveling in seven vehicles including a V–150 APC and unarmored M–35 trucks. The task force was searching for a kidnapped priest but were unable to locate him and withdrew to their vehicles. At 10:30a.m. the task force, stopped by muddy roads, was ambushed by Moro insurgents near Al–Barka. Journalists on the scene claimed up to five hundred armed MILF took part. Calls for air support saw the arrival of initially of one MD–520 and one UH–1H, which arrived around 11:30a.m., and returned to base after the UH–1H was hit by small arms fire. A second strike mission came around 1:20p.m. when two MD–520s and an OV–10, which flew over head without dropping any ordinance. Reports differed as to whether the planes couldn't make contact with the Marines, ran out of fuel, or were ordered back to base. The OV–10s dropped their bombs into the water on their way back to base. The fighting went on through the afternoon. Six rounds of 105mm artillery were fired in support of the Marines, until firing was cancelled, by the AFP/MILF ceasefire committee. In the end the Marines were able to retreat to government positions, a half an hour's march away. Fourteen Marines were killed of which ten were later beheaded and another nine were wounded.

The death of the 14 Marines led to a massive response by the Arroyo government as fresh units were moved into the theater to punish those responsible for the ambush.[29] A list was released having the names of 130 MILF and ASG insurgents who were wanted in relation to the ambush. In early August the son of Isnilon Hapilon was killed in a

NAVSOG commandos displaying an M4 Carbine and MSSR Rifle. (via Timawa)

clash with a Marine patrol. From 2 to 6 August, Marines backed by Special Forces surrounded and took control of Indanan Town.

The hunt for the militants demonstrated several problems. First and foremost was the issue of the peace agreements with the MNLF and the MILF. The Abu Sayyaf took advantage of the agreements and conducted operations out of Moro territory. The AFP was still hampered by the difficulties in differentiating the insurgents, which led to clashes with the MNLF and MILF. An additional issue was that ex–MNLF fighters were serving in the AFP ranks as part of the peace plan, and showed themselves perfectly willing to battle separatist rebels, In the general free for all which followed the AFP raided MNLF positions and clashed with their members. Insurgents provided support to the ASG, often as a local matter as individual commanders supported the militants or as a general matter to protect their own territory from AFP patrols, hunting the ASG. The aggressive tempo of operations led to complaints from personnel. Men conducted constant patrols which mixed with the AFP losses led to complaints from opposition politicians and newspapers.

In a clash a week later, 15 Force Recon trainees, along with a helicopter pilot were killed during an assault against an ASG camp held by close to seventy militants.[30] The Marines were in six teams, made up of one officer and eight enlisted, and linked up with a force

---

30 Five officers and ten enlisted men died in the clash. All were posthumously graduated from the course.

Training operations in war zones is a long established practice among AFP special units, the Scout Rangers have done this for decades.

---

29 Included among the troops sent was the 93rd Marine Security Company which was part of Arroyo's Presidential Security Group (PSG).

LRR commandos with M–4 Carbines equipped with a mix of ACOGs and reflex sights, SR–25s posing in front of one of the handful of operation UH–1s. By the end of 2015 the LRR contained six companies. The manpower for the expansion came from the SFR and SRR. (via Lt. Colonel Dennis Eclarin)

of forty CAFGUs to assault the camp. Moving through a defile they were caught by the Abu Sayyaf who had seized the high ground and ambushed. An MD–520 was hit by enemy fire during the battle, killing the pilot and wounding the co–pilot and the helicopter crashed into the ocean while withdrawing. In the aftermath of the clash the remaining 17 MD–520s were grounded to check for any faults and there was finger pointing over the decision to use trainees to assault a well protected ASG camp.

On 16 August a SRC was flown by C–130 to Jolo to support operations against the Abu Sayyaf. To improve air to ground communications additional FACs were deployed to the south. The FACs were trained pilots and were attached to PA and PMC units. Deploying FACs with ground units was rarely done in operations but the issues stemming from the 10 July clash and the difficulties in coordination prompted deployment.

On 25 September a joint SF/SR/CAFGU patrol clashed with the Abu Sayyaf. In the clash two soldiers, were killed while ten Scout Rangers and militiamen were wounded while inflicting several losses on the ASG. The joint forces clashed with a large militant band in

NAVSOG operators. The one in the centre carries a locally designed M–16 variant Night fighting Weapon System, which is an MSSR fitted with a integral sound suppressor. (via Timawa)

Ungkaya Pukan town on Basilan Island in a several hour clash. In the clash a FAC from the 710th SPOW, attached to 4th SRC, called in air strikes from MD–520s which rocketed Abu Sayyaf positions and finally allowed them to break contact.

CHAPTER 8
BIFF – BACK TO THE PAST

Despite considerable American assistance the conflict showed no sign of ending. The SOF led approach under Oplan Ultimatum had succeeded in weakening the terrorist organization. In 2007, the AFP captured 38 ASG members and killed 127. The ASG was estimated to be down to around 370 members operating primarily on Jolo and Basilan. The group was divided up between a collection of small commanders leading groups of young men who were mostly interested in making money but continued to conduct bombing attacks against civilian targets. The lure of ransom money and loot enabled the ASG to keep their ranks constant. The year 2008 started with a series of bloody setbacks to the ASG. On 31 January a joint force of Marines from MBLT2 and NAVSOG commandos launched a raid to neutralize Wahab Opao in Tawi–Tawi. Opao was killed in the raid but optimistic reports that JI bomb maker Dulmatin and Patek died in the raid

turned out to be false.[31] On 4 February a strike force drawn from the 3rd LRC and NAVSOG clashed with a ASG force under Albader Parad and Abu Pula, who had kidnapped a rice trader, and in the firefight which followed two commandos died along with three militants and eight civilians and several houses were destroyed. On 30 April in response to intelligence regarding a pending attack Task Force Comet launched a night raid using three hundred commandos drawn from the SRR/LRB/FR with support from the PhAF and Marine artillery swept through a JI/ASG camp at Candinamon near Indanan Town killing several. During the raid Isnilon Hapilon was wounded and his was son killed. A minor clash with the MNLF broke out during the operation as the ASG/JI had been based near MNLF territory.

Sporadic clashes broke out between MILF and AFP units during the year as the peace talks bogged down. Throughout the spring men

31 . Dulmatin died in a 2010 Indonesian raid.

A group of NPA insurgents on patrol. (via Albert Grandolini)

An NPA "press conference" (via Albert Grandolini)

SAF Commandos patrolling. SAF battalions are deployed heavily both to conduct independent combat operations and to supervise PMG/RMGs. The unit has been criticized by other AFP units for not being as capable as other elite units in the semi–conventional fighting which often occurs against militant groups. (via Lt. Colonel Dennis Eclarin)

on both sides were killed in minor clashes and raids. In late May the MILF and ASG launched a raid on two Marine bases at Tipo–Tipo In the assault a V–150 was damaged when it hit a mine, wounding ten Marines. Ultimately seventeen Marines of MBLT8 were wounded and two insurgents were killed.

By 2008, the MILF had around 11,500 armed insurgents. During the summer the Philippine Supreme Court blocked a planned peace deal which would have increased the ARMM by 712 villages. In response to the breakdown of peace talks, Commander Ombra Kato the commander of the MILF's 105th Base Command launched a series of attacks. In early July Kato's forces, numbering over a thousand men, began to seize control of villages. The 107th Base Command under Jayon Saligan launched attacks in Sarangani while the 104th Base Command launched attacks in Sultan Kudarat. Kato stated he was acting on his own initiative as a commander to respond to government attacks. On 3 August 2008 a force of 300 MILF insurgents attacked Tipo–Tipo town, killing one Marine of MBLT10 and a civilian and wounding three Marines and one CAFGU. The lack of PhAF air support was evident as the Marines and militiaman were forced to wait for medical evacuation, which was finally provided by a US helicopter. In the initial fighting two OV–10s, two SF–260s, two MD–520s and four UH–1s were on hand. The PhAF forces in North Cotabato were reinforced with two additional OV–10s and two night capable UH–1s. Eventually S–211s were also deployed. AFP counter

attacks quickly recaptured many of the towns. On 14 August a force of 70 insurgents under the command of Commander Adan launched an attack on a CVO outpost located in Matalam, burning and looting several homes before withdrawing. PhAF air strikes killed at least two insurgents according to MILF sources, though the AFP claimed 30 died. Further MILF assaults were turned back by AFP/PNP/CVOs.

In late August the PhAF conducted a major bombing raid on MILF camps at Mamasapano Township in Maguindanao, killing a dozen insurgents in support of operations of the 6th ID by the 40th and 68th IB, 1 and 2nd MIB of the LAD, and 2nd SRB. By the end of operations to capture the MILF camps in Mamasapano Township the 6th ID claimed to have killed 100 insurgents. Bunkers, training camps and IED production factories were seized from the insurgents. The AFP/ SAF conducted raids around Datu Piang in the hopes of capturing Kato.

Commander Bravo, commander of the 102nd Base Command, was targeted by PhAF air strikes and AFP assaults in Lanao del Norte. Camps Bilal and Darapanan were overrun in late August but most of his three hundred fighters escaped. On 11 September the 10th ID including the 66th, 72nd IB, 73rd IB and Scout Rangers swept through Sarangani seizing Buliok Complex. Within a month of fighting some 17 camps had fallen to the AFP. Through the use of light armour, artillery, and CAS the AFP was able to efficiently capture defensive positions, which the insurgents showed little interest in defending.

The insurgents switched to small scale attacks, launched in platoon and company size against towns and small government positions. Several AFP units were ambushed while responding to MILF attacks on soft targets. Because of the Ramadan season and reports of civilian casualities the AFP was under orders to limit the use of supporting firepower when practical. The instructions did not prevent the AFP from making use of supporting to get the better of the insurgents. Though in some engagements the insurgents were able to get too close to allow for the use of CAS, they were still unable to wipe out government units. By October 1,822 homes, eight mosques and six schools had been burned down during the fighting.

With the end of Ramadan, the AFP made more use of heavy firepower in response to the increasing size of rebel bands they encountered. The insurgents typically showed little willingness to hold positions under heavy fire. IEDs were a popular weapon to divert AFP attention as were more conventional terrorist attacks. On 1 November in response to a MILF assault on an AFP outpost near Datu Pinag the elements of three brigades backed by OV–10s launched a series of operations killing twenty–two insurgents. Three days later another dozen insurgents were killed in clashes with the 68th and 64th IB

NPA insurgents cleaning their weapons. (via Albert Grandolini)

NPA insurgents (via Albert Grandolini)

backed by MD–520s and artillery near Tatapan and Pamalian areas, Datu Saudi Ampatuan in Central Mindanao.

While the fighting with the MILF was going on the AFP clashed regularly with ASG bands, including rescuing a group of aid workers and other civilians held for ransom. There was increased use of drones to support tactical operations, enabling ASG bands to be tracked and commandos deployed to raid their camps. Despite AFP pressure the ASG was still able to conduct regular IED attacks and elements of the organization were still active in planning terrorist attacks. MILF units joined the fighting launching attacks on government outposts in Basilan. On 1 December, 300 MILF members attacked MBLT7/CAFGU positions on Lamitan were checked with support from MD–520s and AFVs. The 1st Marine Brigade conducted a series of punitive operations against the MILF on Basilan. Because of the increased fighting troops were sent from Task Force Zamboanga to reinforce operations. Zamboanga City itself was targeted in a failed raid by the MILF–SOG. In fighting near Al–Baraka town on 7 December an OV–10 was damaged and its pilot was wounded by ground fire while providing support of MBLT7 and MBLT10.

MILF insurgents conducted a series of raids around Christmas attacking several villages in Sultan Kudarat and North Cotabato, which in turn led to a series of air strikes and punitive operations against the insurgents. The PhAF attacked larger concentrations of insurgents as they massed for attacks or withdrew after raids. Small scales clashes, raids and bombings followed as the insurgents struck at small government posts and villages. Large numbers of homes were looted and burned in these attacks. Insurgents attacks on villages were typically met with air strikes and government sweeps but the AFP was unable to secure all villages from assault, which led to further militia activity in pro–Government villages.

By early January 2009 the AFP had suffered 42 soldiers and 12 militiamen men killed in 297 clashes since August 2008, while officially being able to confirm the death of 101 insurgents. Rebel morale dropped under the constant pursuit by the AFP and the lack of pay, which led to many surrendering or deserting. Losses continued to mount on both sides as the AFP hunted Kato and other top commanders while the insurgents launched attacks on civilians and small government positions.

In early December 2008 the Marines launched a major operation against the ASG on Basilan. Despite considerable American assistance and aggressive hunting of HVTs the AFP was simply unable to prevent the militants from taking hostages. Over 200 people had been kidnapped since 2003 in 93 incidents. In 2008 alone 50 civilians were taken hostage. This was made more difficult by the money paid out in bribes with money made from kidnapping the through the drug trade

The insurgent closet to the camera has an M–16 with two thirty round magazines welded together, a popular practice among insurgents though the local modified magazines often have reliability problems. (via Albert Grandolini)

and clan ties which allowed the militants to operate. The overstretched military and police could not protect every soft target. JTFC with the support of the US hunted a ASG band under Albader Parad and Radullan Sahiron on Sulu who had captured Red Cross workers. The hunt involved drones and other aerial *reconnaissance* patrols. AFP tactics initially involved keeping the pressure on the militants, fighting small scale clashes and allowing the militants to break contact often without pursuit, gradually there was a push to more decisive clashes aimed at wiping out militant groups. On 16 March it was reported Parad, while leading 50 militants, was wounded in a clash with Special Operations Platoon–3 of MBLT3, which saw three Marines killed and 19 wounded in exchange for six militants. Two sub–commanders were killed but reports of Parad's death turned out to be incorrect.[32] Two hostages were released by the ASG in April, without incident with rumor of ransoms being paid, leaving the band of 50 militants with a single hostage. Clashes with the militant group continued as patrols drawn from elite unit clashed with the hostage takers. On 11 June MBTL4 killed six militants, in Indanan Town in exchange for two killed. On 14 June, a force drawn from the SAF, Marines and CAFGU suffered nine killed, 15 wounded and two APCs damaged in an ASG ambush in Parang Town launched by 40 militants. Heavy firepower forced the militants to withdraw. A joint force of the NAVOG and

---

32 An individual claiming to be Parad called into a radio station and stated he had been wounded in the arm and threatened to behead one of the hostages if the military failed to pull back from the group's lair. Despite the pullback, no hostage was freed.

An army soldier posing next to a NPA tent during a sweep. (via Lt. Colonel Dennis Eclarin)

PNP–Maritime group on junking boat captured an ASG position on Bud Timbahu. The last Red Cross hostage was released on 12 July in Maimbung town, days after the AFP had arrested Parad's wives and after the payment of P50,000 in "cigarette" money. The failure of the militants to secure a large ransom led to defections, bringing the Sulu group from around 200 to 70.

The diverting of AFP resources to fight the MILF and hunt ASG bands allowed other ASG bands to capture more hostages on West Basilan, where a single MBLT and a scattered force of CAFGU were deployed. It was believed around sixty ASG were operating on Basilan. On Basilan the AFP and PNP formed Task Force Trillium to deal with the hostage crisis. The Marines and PNP–PMG/RMGs operated alongside MNLF fighters who worked to clear out area the ASG operated in. The PhAF was normally only able to provide two transport helicopters. The need for manpower was met through the use of militiamen and police auxiliaries to protect soft targets to free up combat troops and mobile PNP units for offensive operations. Several hostages were released unharmed by the militant though one was murdered because the family could not pay a ransom. An air–sea assault launched on 27 May against the hostage takers killed ten militants for the loss of one commando. In the aftermath of an ASG ambush which killed seven PNP troopers a force of 226 SAF trainees on their final test mission was deployed alongside MBLT1 and PNP–RMGs 1519, 1520 and1530 and around 300 other SAF commandos.

Fighting against Kato's force continued despite the hostage drama, as infantry–armor task forces with heavy fire support attacked his

forces in Maguindanao province in late April, clearing out thirteen camps. The insurgents responded with raids against villages, infrastructure targets, and lightly protected government posts. The dwindling number of 15th SW planes were constantly deployed to support tactical operations as was a small number of drones operated by the PA. Causalities were constant but not severe enough to break either side. The AFP was able through the use of superior firepower to seize rebel camps but was unable to decisively annihilate the garrisons, who typically escaped with light losses despite high estimates. In small unit clashes AFP infantry unit were able to call in artillery fire to force the insurgents to break contact. Despite the losses the insurgents continued to conduct IED attacks and raided small military outposts. A cease–fire between the government and MILF force was declared at the end of July, which did not apply to Kato, Bravo and Pangalian. Most of the MILF commanders accepted the ceasefire, despite minor clashes occurring.

A major raid took place on 12 August 2009 which saw 400 commandos[33] strike the bomb making plant in Sitio Kurrelem, Barangay Silangkum in Tipo–Tipo. Initially 50 militants were there but eventually 150 fighters took part as MILF fighters from 114th Base Command joined in the fighting and ambushed 4th SRC who were then reinforced by the 67th MRC which was itself hard pressed.

---

33 4 Scout Ranger Company, 3rd LRC, 61 Force Recon Company, 67 Marine Raider Company, Special Operations Platoon 10 of MBLT10 and the SAF. The raid was begun by the Scout Ranger, LRC, SOP-10 and Force Recon conducting the raid followed by the Marine Raider and SAF.

Because of the close quarters artillery and CAS were not employed. Two UH–1s attempted to remove the wounded but were initially driven off by heavy fire. Commando from the 6th SFC and 1st LRC reinforced the embattled troop. By the time the fighting saw done 23 soldiers were dead and 22 wounded, in exchange for 31 militants. The MILF did not deny taking part but blamed the government and stating it acted in self defense.

The MILF made gains in Maguindanao after of the massacre of 57 political by the Ampatuan Clan, who had provided over 4000 CVOs to the government for years. The SAF/LRB/PMC with the support of light armor and the 15th SW disarmed the heavily armed militiamen which in turn allowed MILF to raid formerly "secure" areas. AFP forces also clashed with ex–CVOs as they attempted to restore order in the province.

Numerous small scale clashes and raids occurred in the hunt for the ASG. On November 3rd a joint MBLT9/CVO force killed five militants including Ridwan Musa, a minor ASG commander, during a meeting engagement on Basilan. The next month a major ASG financer and early member, Adbul Basir Latip was arrested in Indonesia. Despite this and other losses the militants averaged around ten IED strikes a month, conducted regular ambushes and raids, and continued to kidnap civilians. The usual shortages of helicopters dogged pursuit operations, though helicopters were often employed to move LRB raiding parties. With drones and considerable US intelligence support the AFP was able to better target militant camps but despite the losses by the beginning of 2010 the military estimated the ASG still had almost 400 militants. The continued survival of the group was in large part due to the poverty of the region. The problem was the ease in attracting Moro insurgents or the local criminal element to operate under commanders who operated under the ASG banner. The need to raise revenue led to the ASG kidnapping primarily locals of limited means. MILF, MNLF and local thugs conducted similar kidnap for ransom operations, and were typically referred to as ASG. Despite the varied sources of manpower and differing motivations the ASG continued conduct bomb attacks and even raid military camps. The survivors of JI while dangerous were mostly on the run.

In late February 2010, Parad was killed, along with five other militants, in a nighttime Marine raid[34] supported by PhAF CAS in Maimbung town. The Marines claimed 50 militants were present at the time of the raid. One Marine was killed and wounded Marines were withdrawn using an MD–520 helicopter. On 7 March special operations elements of MBLT6 conducted an amphibious raid against the ASG forces on Siasi Sulu killing seven. In the hopes of finishing of the militants on Sulu a battalion sized SF/SR task force was deployed to support the Marines. An airmobile raid was launched on 26 March by Scout Rangers against the camp of Radulan Sahiron in Patikul town, killing one militant. Follow up Ranger/MBLT5 attacks killed several more militants. On 13 April a dozen militants under Puruji Indama dressed as SAF commandos, launched a raid into Isaebela City killing 14, Marines and SAF were rushed to the area and with the support of the elements of the LRB/SRR conducted pursuit operations. By the middle of the year an estimate 50 militants had been killed or captured in 24 clashes.

Small scale fighting continued as the ASG continued to take hostages. On 11 March 2011 the elements of the LRB with the support of UH–1s and MD–520s conducted a raid on Sacol Island after receiving intelligence that Puruji Indama was present and planning an attack against nearby Zamboanga City. The raid failed to capture the militant because the commandos were dropped too far away.

Four months later the ASG militants under Radulan Sahiron inflicted a stinging defeat on a platoon from MBLT11, killing seven and wounded twenty–one. The Marines attempted to raid an ASG camp but were counter attacked and suffered serious losses, while claiming to have killed thirteen militants. Two UH–1s, two MD–520s and a PN gunboat provided support and helped withdraw the wounded. Amazingly despite the losses the militants actually launched around twenty percent more attacks in 2011 then the year before. The AFP claimed there were around 350 militants under the ASG banner.

In October 2011, the forces on Basilan were reorganized, containing the 104th Infantry Brigade and the SOTF–B. SOTF–B had two battalion sized units drawn from SOCOM. The AFP set up SOTF–B partially to remove the Marines from Basilan, who they felt were becoming less effective in the area and partially to showcase SOCOM. The AFP suffered a bloody set back on Oct 18th as nineteen members of the 13th and 19th SFC and Scuba Class #42–11,[35] who were tasked with arresting Hassan Asnawi[36], were killed in a clash with the MILF 114th Base Command on Al–Barka town in Basilan, in exchange for seven MILF members. Part of the SF unit was deployed from naval ships offshore while the other was moving on foot. The SF and ASG clashed near MILF territory which brought the insurgents into the battle. Artillery fire was late and inaccurate and the 15th SW arrived too late. Towards the end of the clash two UH–1s dropped a unit of Rangers to support the SF. The MILF claimed the AFP failed to inform them of the operation.. Clashes followed with the MILF ambushing a convoy two days later on Zamboanga Sibugay. To reinforce operations a SRC and elements of the LRB were deployed to the area. The AFP responded by attacking the 113rd Base Command in Zamboanga Sibugay with artillery and airstrikes. PA/PNP troops with the support of armor pushed in and seized control of several villages. JSOTF–P helped bring the PhAF into the 21st Century as PhAF OV–10s were fitted with guided bombs with covert American assistance and were used in a major strike on JI and ASG militants on 2 February 2012.[37] The regional JI leader Marwan initially reported killed with two other leaders and a dozen other militants in a nighttime OV–10 strike, supported by US Scan Eagle Drones, employing four GPS guided bombs near Parang Town on Jolo. It was later discovered that Marwan had not been killed in the air strike.

In late August 2011, Kato officially broke away from the MILF forming the Bangsamoro Islamic Freedom Fighters (BIFF), initially with around 1,000 militants formerly of the 104th and 105th Base Commands. This put Kato and his forces outside of MILF protection but created the risk of disaffected MILF flocking to his banner. Operations against the BIFF went on as AFP units in 2012 attacked their camps and attempted to kill or capture their leadership. The BIFF launched raids of its own attacking post and villages. The movement had a few hundred full time fighters and was unable to hold its camps and villages against AFP attacks. . Combined arms punitive operations were launched in early 2014 against BIFF insurgents, seizing several camps and killing over 50 insurgents. The MILF supported the AFP actions but there was criticism from MNLF linked commanders.

Talks with the MILF continued with Malaysian assistance as both sides moved closer to agreement. The AFP and MILF tried to avoid conflict in the last few years, but tragically men on both sides were killed. A quixotic attempt by Nur Misauri to derail the talks with an

---

34 The Marines were drawn from SOP-7, two recon companies and a class of Scout Sniper trainees.

35 Both companies were under the 4SFB and part of Special Operations Task Force Basilan (SOTF-B). The 41 man task force was made up of trainees on their final missions. The mission was

36 He was deputy commander of Base Command 114 and was wanted for the beheading of Marines in 2007

37 At least twenty-two GPS guided bombs were provided the PhAF from November 2010.

Scout Rangers posing next to an M–101 during anti–insurgent operations on Basilian. (via Lt. Colonel Dennis Eclarin)

assault on Zamboangao City in the summer of 2013 was crushed by a combined force drawn from the LRB, PMC and SAF. Finally in 2014 a peace deal was signed with the MILF expanding regional autonomy, which was threatened almost as soon as it was signed.

In January 2015, 44 SAF commandos were killed in clashes with the MILF and BIFF during a raid at Mamasapano which led to the death of JI mastermind Marwan. In the lead up to the US supported operation the 392 man SAF detachment, drawn from two battalions, failed to coordinate with the MILF which had three base camps in the area, the PA which had armour and artillery within close range or PhAF which had two SF–260s and two UH–1s nearby. Mawaran was killed in his hut by members of the 84th SAC but the sounds of battle alarmed Moro insurgents who came to the area. The blocking force made up from the 55th SAC was hit hard by MILF insurgents. The SAF V–150s with the remaining three SAF troopers were unable to over forward to support the two embattled SACs as the main force came under attack. Poo coordination prevented fire support from being marshaled. A combined arms task force built around the 45 IB, with six Simba APCs, rescued the survivors. This clash reaffirmed the dangers of operating with light infantry basically alone when the insurgents can quickly grow in numbers and are as well–equipped as comparable platoon and company sized formations. Punitive operations were launched against the ASG and BIFF spearheaded by SOCOM and the Marines with the usual artillery/armour/PhAF phalanx. The BIFF though hit hard by AFP offensives by the end of 2015 was still conducting raids against civilian targets and sniped at government posts. In fighting on Sulu during 2015 the AFP/PNP claimed to have killed 133 ASG militants, wounded an additional 164, captured 53 small arms and arrested thirteen militants but only

Two well armed Scout Ranger officers in the aftermath of the 2014 Zamboabgoa clashes. Note the 76mm equipped Scorpion light–tank. (via Lt. Colonel Dennis Eclarin)

recovered twelve dead militants. Despite these figures 234 militants were reported to remain in the field. As of the date of print clashes continue with the BIFF and ASG while talks with the MILF over regional autonomy continue.

NPA Front 2000 – 2014
The NPA has survived the fall of the Berlin Wall despite having practically no external support. The insurgents rely heavily on forcing businesses and farmers to pay protection money and are involved in the drug trade. The movement suffered serious setbacks in the 1990s but survived, often in areas which had the most deeply entrenched

political dynasties. The NPA relies on manpower as diverse as college radicals, career criminals all the way to "hill tribes". Small units of insurgents are spread around the republic; in 2001 there were 35 NPA fronts in Mindanao alone and 70 out of the nation's 79 provinces had NPA fronts. Poor governance and the military shortcomings have allowed the NPA continue to influence areas. On and off peace talks between the RP and the NPA have been going on since 1995 with little chance of success. The NPA even refuses to provide the names of negotiators until after they are arrested by the AFP/PNP, attempting to use the stalled talks to free cadres.

In 2002, the AFP put Oplan Bantay into effect. Building on decades of COIN experience the AFP sought to use regular units to clear out rebel fronts then deploy SOTs to reassert government control. CAFGUs would be raised from the cleared areas. Various anti–poverty initiatives were launched. On a darker note extra judicial activities continued with the AFP and political elites killing leftist activists who were supporting the insurgents. Despite AFP actions the NPA actually increased its coverage. The movement "affected" 1969 villages in 2001 a number which had actually grown by around five hundred two years later. This was despite the government having swept through hundreds of villages.

Unlike the often semi conventional fighting with the Moros the war with the NPA remained one of small units. Despite control of the skies and superior firepower the insurgents often broke even with the AFP/PNP. From 15 December 2003 to 9 June 2004; 148 soldiers and 121 policemen died fighting the NPA in exchange for 285 insurgents killed, 159 surrendered and 85 arrested. The clashes broke almost fifty–fifty with the NPA initiating 128 and the government some 121. Remote outposts were easy to raid and made tempting sources of weapons and ammunition.

The Army's Scout Rangers and Special Forces also have been heavily involved in conducting operations against the insurgents. Despite the pressing needs against Islamic militants the LRB has also taken part in deployments against the Communists. Detachments conducted raids against NPA camps. The need to deploy elite forces to other parts of the country drained away the available forces to clear actively hunt rebel detachments. Small detachments of the PhAF were deployed to support major clearing operations and the pursuit of rebel bands after major raids. Operating in tandem with elite units small numbers of helicopters and OV–10s often allowed units to overcome NPA bands.

The 2nd SRB with air support provided by the 15th SW captured a major NPA command center in Surigao Sur killing four communist insurgents in May 2005. With the advantage of air support and superior training mixed with the element of surprise the NPA were swept off the field within an half an hour and retreated leaving the Scout Rangers in control of the camp. In the pursuit the total of dead insurgents reached thirteen as the Scout Rangers with support of army artillery and air support chased down the survivors. Elements of the 8th SFB clashed with the NPA in June 2005. The clash went on for more than an hour as the Special Forces backed by airpower inflicted numerous causalities on the insurgents, including taking two prisoners. Elements from the 15th SW and 205th TOW supported the operation.

Oplan Bantay was altered to have a greater focus on hunter killer operations in concert with the SOTs. In mid–2005 the military announced plans to change the composition of forces facing the guerilas. Too many soldiers were tied down in small numbers on static defensive assignments. Of some 75,000 soldiers facing the NPA, the majority were in small units spread across the countryside. These small detachments were easy targets and prevented the army from rapidly massing forces against NPA bands allowing them easy escapes after attacks. Sixty–one battalions were to be freed up from static missions leaving sixteen for defensive activities. The reality was somewhat different as lack of mobility and continued security needs limited the number of units available at any one time for offensive operations.

According to government figures from 1984 through to the start of 2006 some 40,000 had died in the war against the NPA. During 2006, the NPA increased assaults on government positions. The NPA saw the time good for increased attacks with the stated hope of overthrowing the government. In Mindanao the 35th Guerilla Front, from January 2005 to the end of April 2006 had conducted, according to its commanders, 412 tactical offensives in nineteen of twenty–five provinces and some two hundred towns, villages and cities. The insurgents claimed to have captured some three hundred weapons from the AFP, PNP and militia groups. They claimed six major attacks in Mindanao against police stations, two against militia posts and five large scale ambushes inflicting, according to the insurgents, 304 troops killed and 200 wounded. The NPA claimed to retain 120–130 fronts, groups of several towns with communist shadow governments, spread across the country. The NPA had dropped from around 12,000 men in 2000–2001 down to some 7,000–8,000 men by 2006. Despite the losses the NPA presence had grown from 2001, from 1,960 communities with a rebel presence to 2,178 by 2005. In mid–2006 the overly ambitious plans to defeat the NPA by 2008 were scrapped. In fact things had gone bad for the AFP, more soldiers than guerilas were killed in the first half of the year. From 1 January to 27 June, 104 soldiers were killed compared to 87 insurgents. The difference in losses was due to the NPA use of IEDs and ambushes, and losses to non combat units such as medical troops conducting civil–affairs operations. On a positive note the AFP claimed to have captured (155) more weapons from the NPA than it lost (65).

Police stations remained tempting targets due to their scattered dispositions and small garrisons. By April of 2006 according to the PNP 97 firearms, including 74 rifles, had been captured during raids on police stations by the NPA, compared to 75 the year prior. Raids against police stations were short and broken off if there was fierce resistance from the defenders. Some fell without losses to either side as insurgents would use disguises to enter and quickly disarm the police station and withdraw before reinforcements arrived.

President Arroyo called on the AFP and PNP to run the NPA to ground as part of a general campaign in Central and Southern Luzon. Additional units were deployed to conduct attacks on the NPA infrastructure, including their extortion group. Breaking the extortion gangs was an important goal of AFP/PNP operations. Both to cripple the rebel financing and to show the civilian population the government could protect them as part of this push business records were scoured to see which companies were paying off the NPA for protection.

In 2006, the PNP and AFP came to an agreement on troop dispositions in the counter insurgency conflict. Since 1990 the PNP had been a supporting service to the struggle. They agreed to split the task, gaining equal responsibility; PNP units would control operations in the urban areas while the AFP would control operations in the countryside. The PNP was expanded its COIN role focusing initially on urban areas, yet still maintained a large rural presence. The PNP also formed auxiliary police units, similar to the CAFGU, to protect local communities from rebel attacks. In addition, SACs were deployed to support PNP operations, conducting training for local police and engaging in raids against NPA camps.

At the end of January 2006 solders backed by MD–520s conducted an assault against the NPA killing a reported eighteen insurgents near

A SOCOM operator equipped with the elderly though powerful M–14 rifle during the operations in Zamboanga city. (via Lt. Colonel Dennis Eclarin)

Santa Ignacia, a town around 80 miles north of Manila. A force of over 20 insurgents had begun to organize for an assault on the town and its telecommunications center, when intelligence alerted the army who with the PhAF attacked the NPA force. Four of the bodies were flown by UH–1H to be viewed by onlookers. Major clashes like this were rare, more common were IED strikes, raids, and small scale ambushes. With the major effort to break the ASG the AFP was forced to remove assets from the war against the NPA. There were steady clashes between the NPA and the AFP as the NPA remained able to raid at will. During the first half of 2007 only two NPA fronts had been destroyed, far short of the planned 18. By the beginning of 2008 there were reported to be 5700 NPA members under arms operating in 87 fronts, each front covering around five to six towns and villages. Even in areas deemed secured the insurgents would sometimes conduct attacks to discredit the AFP, even if the NPA was unable to reorganize in those areas.

President Benigno Aquino III launched Plan Bayanihan in 2010 aimed at hearts and minds and attempting to improve local governance with the aim of finishing the conflict by 2016. Part of this plan was to reign in extra–judicial killing and improve treatment of civilians. Between 2001 and 2008 it was estimated by human rights groups that as many as 800 extra–judicial killings of left wing activists and NPA supporters occurred. The PNP countered by claiming the death tallies were inflated, that most of the deaths were not connected to politics, and that the NPA was conducting purges on its own memberships. Both sides pointed the finger at the other for the deaths of tribal

chieftains in areas where the NPA is active. Alleged Sparrow Units murdered former rebels, CAFGUs, and suspected informants. These new Sparrow Units were three man teams drawn from the NPA Fronts and deployed to areas to carry out specific assignments. Weakness in the PNP's ability to provide security and bring criminal charges against insurgents has continued to hamper the campaign.

Despite these offensives the NPA in the provinces were able to launch raids and continued to extort local businesses. Internally the extortion campaign has hurt morale with defections coming from insurgents complaining of the life styles of higher ranking cadres. AFP/PNP pressure has been able to hamper NPA extortion which saw a serious drop in 2011, a year which saw 341 members killed or captured. Despite the figures the NPA launched 447 attacks that year, including 178 against the AFP/PNP. In the summer of 2011 the AFP conducted a series of large scale operations in Agusan del Sur province to clear out two NPA fronts. The 15th SW was deployed to cover an airmobile raid by the 402th IB which spearheaded the assault. Eventually an entire brigade was in operations against over one hundred insurgents who melted into the countryside. Similar operations occurred throughout the fall as the fighting shifted to Agusan del Norte with Scout Rangers and the 15th SW raiding suspected NPA camps. Operations like this ran individual fronts to ground and then cleared the way for SOTs and the PNP to help reestablish government control.

With the MILF peace process moving forward around sixty percent of AFP units on Mindanao are deployed against the NPA. By 2015, around 4,000 armed insurgents remain in the field supported by extortion, taxation, but with a surprising degree of support in some rural areas. Much of the luster of a Maoist revolution is over but the NPA remains able to tap into rural discontent to allow them to keep a force in the field despite the losses they have suffered and the regular trickle of desertions. The NPA remains strongest in Mindanao and at least 800 members in at least 24 Fronts, though the NPA claims 49 Fronts on Mindanao. According to government sources by 2015 the number of NPA indicated attacks had dropped to 119, down from 168 in 2011; the NPA in turn claimed 500 NPA tactical offensives in 2015 and 350 in 2011. The NPA is still able to mount platoon and company sized raids on police stations and soft targets such as mines, logging facilities and farms; even taking soldiers and policemen as prisoners. Government sweeps are able to seize bomb making facilities and rebel encampments and with the greater number of pro–government militias and increased police presence the NPA is being squeezed.

Regular announcements about the defeat of the NPA by a particular date have failed. The NPA not only remains active but is capable of conducted raids on PNP posts, setting off regular IED strikes and conducting ambushes. On the other hand the organization at present stands a miniscule chance of over–throwing the government or even seizing control of large swathes of territory.

CONCLUSION

As the armed forces of a developing nation fighting on and off for 70 years the AFP has had to adapt to facing insurgents and militants spread over the second largest archipelago in the world. Plans to modernize with a focus on conventional warfare have been constantly delayed by the needs of the civil war. The AFP is currently a predominantly light infantry force supported by light armour in the form of wheeled and tracked APCs, elderly though still effective artillery and a small air force and navy. The rise in the use of IEDs has not led to the deployment of mine protected vehicles like in the US or South Africa and AFP/PNP unis have suffered a steady drain of losses from IED strikes.

COIN textbook methods are effectively stillborn in face of corruption, entrenched political elites, provincial warlordism, and rampant poverty. Insurgent groups have easy access to small arms and a ready supply of disenfranchised men and women who are prepared to fight. The AFP has relied heavily on a mix of large scale firepower intensive sweeps combined, raids by elite forces, and extra–judicial tactics targeting alleged rebel supporters. SOTs while conducting traditional hearts and minds tasks have also worked hand in hand with alleged death squads to successfully wipe out rebel infrastructure in the provinces.

The revolt in the 1950s was highly localized and was broken by a combination aggressive small unit actions, large scale sweeps, provincial militias run by the very political elites the revolt was fought against, and the targeting of Huk leadership. The Marcos Regime had the misfortune of facing two reasonably well led insurgent groups, one of which was well supported by Libya, in a conflict which was waged across the republic. Fortunately for the government the MNLF at times decided to fight set piece battles, allowing the AFP to inflict serious losses on the insurgents. The NPA was able to benefit from this diversion of resources which might have otherwise strangled it in the cradle. Under the Marcos Regime the threat grew to such an extent that it overwhelmed the ability of the regime to maintain suppress the revolts, and instead such high handed methods served to slow the spread of revolt down. Today it is a movement in decline.

The inability of the military to break the back of the insurgencies has left political solutions as the only viable route for the time being with the major separatist groups. In conventional fighting the AFP maintains a significant advantage over the insurgents. Attempts by insurgents to hold ground in the face of government assaults have failed repeatedly in the face of superior government firepower. Unlike insurgencies in Algeria, the former Rhodesia or Afghanistan the insurgent groups lack safe base areas located in neighboring nations and a reliable source of external support. Since the 1970s the AFP has been faced with a conflict spread across the Archipelago which has in turned limited its ability to mass forces. The mix of small unit strikes and large scale sweeps backed with firepower has been able to maintain a stalemate. Various peace deals, giving over territory to the insurgents, keep MNLF and MILF forces reasonably pacified, with major disturbances dealt with through punitive campaigns. Such large scale punitive operations while expensive in terms of ammunition and fuel used are regarded as far safer sand send a definitive message. These offensives overwhelm insurgent positions, capture villages, and seize arms and ammunition but often fail to inflict substantial losses on the insurgents or break their will or ability to fight. Often the insurgents can scatter and launch attacks in different areas and raid small government outposts.

The war against the ASG forced changes on the AFP leading to the expansion of SOCOM to almost 20,000 men. The ASG as a criminal organization remains strong despite the loss of most of its veteran commanders. The ready flow of young men with few job opportunities has allowed the group to survive as a loose criminal organization as opposed to the Islamist group it had once been poised to become. The members have ready access to small arms and make money from extortion, kidnapping and the drug trade. In more developed nations a small criminal organization would not warrant air strikes but the instability and huge number of armed insurgents means a band of a one to two dozen can expand to a company sized force within a short time.

The AFP habitually operated in large numbers on patrols out of the experience of the war against the MNLF. The ASG operates in small groups, forcing the AFP to do the same both to cover large distances and to move unseen. Intelligence on militant movements is also provided by local informants, double agents inside the ranks of these organizations, and radio intercepts. AFP long duration patrols track small groups and called in air strikes, conducted direct action raids on small groups and where possible called in larger units. Greater use of night operations by the AFP, on the ground and in the air, has successfully kept the pressure on the ASG and allows the AFP to run small militant bands to ground. The operations against the ASG often occur alongside in with operations against insurgent forces. The AFP has also relied heavily on elite units to take the fight to insurgent forces and spearhead punitive operations. Superior training, equipment and through the deployment of higher tech assets these units undertake operations against HVTs and spearhead assaults against well defended targets.

On major operations elements of SOCOM serve alongside PA/PMC infantry battalions and armoured units in sweeps of insurgent camps. In semi–conventional fighting battalions of the PA and PMC have the weight and firepower to seize insurgent towns and the numbers to hold newly acquired territory. When the elements can be brought together this mix of elite light infantry backed with relatively heavy support has shown itself able to seize insurgent held towns and camps. The use of elite units, unsupported by light armour and artillery, to strike well defended camps and rebel bases has led at times to serious losses, especially in cases where the number of militants was underestimated and where air support often unavailable. Many of these incidents have involved student trainees on test missions and typically occurred in areas close to MILF or MNLF camps, which were not the intended targets, allowing for the rapid reinforcement of militants; situations which arguably were more suited to heavier formations.

The PhAF has shown itself to be vital for operations, for CAS and for transportation, despite the declining size of its force. The presence of even a handful of planes can tip the balance in favor of AFP units, while the absence of such support has led to tragic incidents. With small detachments forward based around the south the PhAF is able to take part in the majority of offensive operations and is able to respond to insurgent attacks. From its numeric peak in the 1970s it possesses less than three dozen ground attack platforms, around fifty transport helicopters and around two or three operational C–130s at any time. The large scale airmobile operations which were a fixture during the Vietnam War or Algeria are rare, limited to generally a few helicopters carrying small raiding parties drawn from elite units. Insurgent units are often able to withdraw after raids and ambushes without being cut off by airmobile units, due to the shortage of helicopters. There are ambitious plans for PhAF modernization, including the recent acquisition of South Korean made F/A–50 light fighters and additional transport assets, but the PhAF struggles to keep even its current fleet in the air.

The NPA while in a serious decline remains a serious nuisance, despite the long–shot odds of it seizing power. Through a mix of limited popular support and revolutionary terror the organization has survived for forty years and maintains contacts with various left wing student groups and even legitimate human rights groups. Government SOTs and militia holding villages, economic development in rural provinces and the killing or capturing of insurgent leadership and has seriously harmed the movement. Even with only 3,000 men under arms the organization conducts almost daily operations; raiding and ambushing government units across the republic, and runs lucrative extortion rackets to finance its operations.

Over the last several years the insurgent and militant attacks have dropped somewhat and with the MILF peace treaty, provided it holds, the AFP should have more resources to deploy against the NPA, BIFF and ASG. At present the BIFF and ASG are themselves a small threat to the integrity of the Republic and both have been hit hard by AFP punitive but with the ongoing peace talks the situation remains tense. In the next few years it will be seen if the Moro peace treaties hold or if they collapse, continuing the cycle of violence.

SELECTED BIBLIOGRAPHY

Abuza, Zachary, *Militant Islam in Southeast Asia: Crucible of Terror*, (Lynne Rienner Publishers, 2003). 978–1588262370

Chapman, William, *Inside the Philippine Revolution*, (W. W Norton and Company, 1987). 978–0393024616

Conboy, Ken, *South–East Asian Special Forces*, (London: Osprey Publishing, 1991). 978–1855321069

Davis, Leonard, *Revolutionary Struggle in the Philippines*, (Palgrave Macmillan, 1989). 978–0312028183

Ferrer, Antonieto, *Kauswagan to the Fall of Abubakar*, (AM Cleofe Prints, 2002). 978–9719260608

Kessler, Richard, *Rebellion and Repression in the Philippines*, (New Haven: Yale University Press, 1989). 978–0300051308

McKenna, Thomas, *Muslim Rulers and Rebels: Everyday Politics and Armed Separatism in the Southern Philippines*, (University of California Press, 1998). 978–0520210158

Jones, Gregg, *Red Revolution*, (Westview Press Inc., 1989). 978–0813306445

Kudeta: The Challenge to Philippine Democracy, (Philippine Center for Investigative Journalism. 1990). 978–9718686003

McCoy, Alfred, *Closer Than Brothers: Manhood in the Philippine Military Academy*, (Yale University Press, 1999). 978–0300077650

McCoy, Alfred, *Policing America's Empire: The United States, The Philippines and the Rise of the Surveillance State*, (University of Wisconsin Press, 2009). 978–0299234140

Pobre, Cesar and Quilop, Raymund, *In Assertion of Sovereignty*, (Armed Forces of the Philippines Office of Strategic Studies, 2008). 978–971–94342–0–7

Reid, Robert and Guerrero, Eileen, *Corazon Aquino and the Brushfire Revolution*, (Louisiana State University Press, 1995). 978–0807119808

Valeriano, Napolean and Bohannan, Chris, *Counter Guerilla Operations: The Philippine Experience*, (Praeger, 2006). 978–0275992668

Vitug, Marties Danguiland and Glenda, Gloria, *Under the Crescent Moon: Rebellion in Mindanao*, (Ateneo Center for Social Policy and Public Affairs, 2000). 978–9719167976

ACKNOWLEDGMENTS

This book is a result of cooperation with a number of individuals from around the Philippines and elsewhere, who generously helped with background and insider knowledge, relevant information and expertise. There is little doubt it would have been impossible to prepare without their kind help, and the author would like to express his special gratitude to every one of them – though this will have to happen in private.

Some of those I am free to offer my thanks in public are the Gonzales family in Cabanatuan City. Many other persons provided invaluable support, primarily through supplying their own photographs and for this I would like to thank to the gentlemen of Timawa Defense Forum for allowing me to use photographs and for much help over the years. I would especially like to thank both Albert Grandolini and Marc Koelich from France for providing photographs and for helping me out over the last decade as well. I would like to thank Lieutenant Colonel Dennis Eclarin for providing me with both images and information during our meeting in Quezon City. I would like to thank my parents for all their support over the years. Last but not least, I would like to extend my thanks to Tom Cooper in Austria, who helped me get this project off the ground and mentored me over the last decade.

ABOUT THE AUTHOR

Aaron Morris, from the United States, is a licensed attorney and military historian residing in Washington DC. He developed an interest in armed conflicts in the developing world while a high school student, and specializes in medieval Central and South Asian History, post–Second World War, South East Asian and African military history. A chance visit to the United States Marine Corps museum with his father in the 9th grade peaked his interest about the ongoing civil war in the Philippines. Aaron has travelled extensively to the Philippines during and after his college studies and has been working on this project on and off for over a decade. Aaron has published two magazine articles on the Philippine Air Force's history and contribution to the civil war. The book *Counterinsurgency in Paradise* is his first publication through Helion Publishing.